Tropical
Desserts

Tropical Desserts

Recipes for Exotic Fruits, Nuts, and Spices

Andrew MacLauchlan with Donna K. Flynn

Foreword by Mark Miller

Macmillan USA

MACMILLAN
A Simon & Schuster Macmillan Company
1633 Broadway
New York, NY 10019-6785

Library of Congress Cataloging-in-Publication Data available on request.
ISBN: 0-02-861300-7

Manufactured in the United States of America

10 9 8 7 6 5 4 3 2 1

Interior Design by George J. McKeon

Contents

Foreword

Tropical and dessert are two words that incite pleasure for all of us. The word tropical connotes warm, silky breezes and sandy beaches with turquoise waters and swaying palms and a simpler, more romantic lifestyle. The taste of the tropics are strong—ripe, fragrant, juicy—tastes that immediately satisfy. The tropics are our lost Eden.

The word dessert conjures up pleasurable memories also—birthday cakes, warm apple pies, hot fudge sundaes, chocolate soufflés, butterscotch pudding, mince meat pie, brownies—dessserts are foods of celebration, rewards, holidays, special dinner occasions, extraordinary sweet and rich treats. The desserts that I grew up with and came to expect in restaurants were designed from an old concept—one of rarity. The eating of rare and costly foods—in this case, sugar, which was vary rare at one time—was eaten at times of holidays and feasts in the homes of the wealthy, conferring status and a sense of abundance.

The best dessert was therefore the richest one, because it was more costly and special. So desserts using lots of cream, sugar, butter, white flour became the ultimate desserts. There's nothing wrong with rich desserts if they are limited to a few times per year. Now, though, more people eat in restaurants on a weekly or daily basis where rich desserts are often served. We all like to reward ourselves for our hard work with a little sweet and we have come to expect life to be a little more pleasurable on a daily basis.

In the old world of desserts, tropical flavors were unavailable. With the European discovery of the new worlds and new plants, more tropical flavors like coffee, vanilla and cocoa were introduced to and utilized in traditional desserts. Although vanilla, coffee, and cocoa are all tropical plants, the tropical flavors were masked by too much sugar or butter or cream. The real tropical experience was absent.

Enter a new world with Andrew MacLauchlan's new book, *Tropical Desserts*. All the masks are coming off, and the main character on the stage is no longer sugar or cream but luscious mangoes, fragrant ginger, and enticing passion fruits. Each recipe puts the flavors first and the cream and butter second. These desserts are more intense—a lot of them depend on ripe tropical fruits with their enveloping, complex perfumes.

In these desserts, we can discover the Eden that was lost—simpler flavors that shine brightly like the midday sun on a tranquil isle. Flavors that soothe the spirit like the smell of night-blooming flowers. Flavors that are lacquered in bright colors like the fiery sunsets on tropical isles. Flavors that make us feel alive—that excite the senses— not smother them. These desserts are not "floating islands." They are tropical storms with flavors and textures that sweep over our tongues in a gale of delight.

Andrew has taken some old familiar favorites and given them new twists—a roasted banana in cream becomes more intense and "banana-y" in a coconut cream cake. He creates intriguing flavor combinations like clove and grapefruit. He creates whimsy with a Fourth of July Cinnamon

Red-Hot Angel Food Cake. There are so many to choose from—all delicious.

These are desserts that one can enjoy every day and not worry about dietary sinning. They are fresher, lighter, and healthier—mostly based on nature's most natural intense flavors—fruits. Fruits that through modern technology arrive ripe and bountiful with juice and natural sweetness. These desserts are better for children—not only are they healthier, but the tropical tastes will expand their palates and they will depend less on sugar and fat for pleasure. They will learn to eat healthier and get more pleasure from eating a variety of foods.

Too often we think we have to deprive ourselves of something to be saved from it. In this book, Andrew includes the following quote from Oscar Wilde, with which I agree: "The real way to overcome temptation is to give in to it." But we must pick our temptations wisely. *Tropical Desserts* has a temptation on every page and you don't have to worry about giving in.

These are desserts that are full of joy, love, and excitement—desserts that will give you and your family and friends pleasure for a long time and desserts that, no matter what your culinary skill, you will find rewarding.

Mark Miller, Owner, Coyote Cafe, Red Sage
Author, *Indian Market Cookbook*
Co-author, *Flavored Breads*

Introduction

My personal explorations of tropical produce were inspired by travels and periods of residence in Mexico and West Africa. Living in a tropical region opens one's eyes to the enormous possibilities of tropical products, as you reach greater understanding of their indigenous lands, seasonal growth patterns, and usage in ethnic cuisine. I think foods are best appreciated when understood in light of their rich cultural contexts, and my exposure to tropical fruits in West Africa led me to experiment with them in my professional dessert-making and baking. I remember my first sight of an enormous, sweeping mango tree, with its dark green leaves fluttering and its branches dripping with hundreds of red and green mangoes bouncing in the savanna breeze. Mango trees are sources of sustenance as well as shelter from the penetrating rays of the equatorial sun, providing cool spots of shade for passersby and small gatherings of friends. And I'll never forget my first taste of a sweet cashew fruit—still commercially unavailable in the United States due to its perishability—whose precious flavor is reminiscent of apples and grapes combined.

I lived in Bénin in 1993 and 1994 with my wife, Donna. She was awarded a Fulbright scholarship to conduct anthropological research. I assisted Donna and worked as an artist, painting tropical landscapes and scenes from daily life. One day while I was living in Bénin, West Africa, I was driving my motorcycle through the bush to my village after visiting the post office twenty miles away when a friend, John, flagged me down as I passed by his farm. He saw me approaching and stood waving in the dirt road to make sure I stopped. When I dismounted the bike, he led me into the heart of his plantain fields where we were surrounded by the towering ten- to fourteen-foot-tall herbaceous plants. They provided cool, leafy shade from the hot noonday sun. John chose one of the tallest plantain trees and used his machete to chop it down at its base, close to the ground. Then he cut off a four-foot-long branch that held around forty large green plantains, and offered them to me. What an incredible gift! We stuffed the plantain branch, with its protruding tight bunches of fruit, into an old burlap sack and strapped it onto the back of my motorcycle. Donna and I had plantains to eat and share with other friends for a month afterward—we pounded green ones flat and fried them Cuban style, and enjoyed them in the mornings caramelized on top of our oatmeal.

When we lived in West Africa, we ate according to the seasons. Mangoes, papayas, cashew fruits, and pineapples were each available at different times of the year. Bananas were generally available year-round, but the varieties always changed: ladyfingers, Cavendish, and plantains were in season at alternating times. When using tropical fruits, you should always keep seasonality in mind. Some fruits called for in these recipes are available only in fall and winter, while others are around in the summer. Because seasons in parts of the southern hemisphere are opposite our own—summer in subtropical New Zealand blooms when snow falls in Vermont—many tropical fruits are available during our colder months, making winter an ideal time to experiment with the diverse varieties. Tropical climates also have annual rainy seasons, when certain trees flourish and produce fruit intensively for only a few months out of the year.

Shopping in supermarkets where there's a never-ending supply of our favorite fruits always on the shelves, it's easy to forget that fruits are seasonal produce. But chances are you'll remember this when looking for many of the fruits called for in these recipes, whose availability in our stores is still largely determined by seasonality in their tropical homes. Some tropical and subtropical fruits that are widely cultivated around the world and in the United States, such as bananas and coconuts, are available year-round. Other, more exotic ones are usually very seasonal. My best advice to you is: If you see a tropical or subtropical fruit that intrigues you, buy it! If you think about it too long, it may be gone when you go back looking for it.

The range of produce in our supermarkets continues to grow, with increasing imports of less common tropical fruits, like passion fruits, mangoes, and guavas. With this cookbook, I want to encourage you to experiment with both well-known and unusual tropical and subtropical products by providing you with examples of simple but innovative desserts, pastries, and breads. In many of these recipes, the ingredients may seem exotic but the preparations will be familiar. By integrating tropical fruits, nuts, and spices into everyday cookies, cakes, ice creams, and breads, you can reinvigorate traditional American recipes with the new diversity of produce available in the United States today.

In developing these recipes, I've sought to keep the preparations and techniques as simple as possible while maintaining strong and rich flavor, allowing any cook to enjoy the intense floral and fruity flavors of the tropics. Although I adapt tropical products to classic European and American dessert forms and recipes, I seek to maintain the integrity of the fruits, nuts, and spices by pairing them with each other and offering suggestions for complementary flavor combinations. We've long enjoyed some of these tropical combinations, like orange and chocolate, coffee and banana, or papaya and lime. Others are newer to us and more contemporary but equally delicious, like mango and ginger, coconut and guava, persimmon and dates, or tamarind and almond.

I hope this cookbook serves as a source, guide, and inspiration to you in your own exploration and experimentation with tropical and subtropical fruits, nuts, and spices. Let the mysteries and pleasures of pungent spices and luscious ripe fruits lead you to new culinary discoveries, as you travel around the world with the diverse foodstuffs and flavors presented in these recipes. Enjoy them as I do, and harvest the treasures of the tropics!

Tracing the Trade Routes of Tropical Fruits and Spices

The abundant tropical and subtropical fruits now available in the United States have long and revealing histories, telling us stories about their native homes, indigenous usage, European travels and imperialistic conquests, and commercial development. Only relatively recently, in the past century, have European and American societies gained consistent access to some of our favorite fruits, like bananas or pineapples. By the late 1800s, most Europeans and North Americans had heard of tropical fruits and likely seen pictures of them, but only a privileged, wealthy few had the opportunity of tasting the luscious and diverse varieties. Britain's King George III grew pineapples and oranges in his famous Kew gardens, and European and American elites with financial means were able to purchase some tropical fruits from limited imports or from plant collectors who experimented with cultivation. But most Westerners could only imagine the delicious flavors of bananas, coconuts, figs, grapefruits, guavas, mangoes, papayas, pineapples, and the abundant other tropical and subtropical fruits, based on the stories of travelers and adventurers who told of the sweet fruits and their "mysterious" healthful benefits.

Oranges, lemons, and limes were some of the first tropical fruits to be adopted by European countries and the United States. Oranges were carried to Spain, Portugal, and other sunny European countries from southern China and Southeast Asia, where they had been important dietary elements since at least 4000 B.C. Columbus brought oranges, limes, and lemons to America in 1493 and planted them in his colony of Hispaniola (Haiti). Twenty years later, in 1513, Puerto Rican colonial governor Ponce de León landed on the Florida peninsula, near current-day Jacksonville, where he planted orange and lemon trees. Bananas were introduced into Haiti from the Canary Islands by a Spanish missionary priest named Friar Tomás de Berlanga. They originated in India, where they were regarded as the "fruit of the wise" and consumed green by Hindu ascetics as proof of their austerity. Bananas are one tropical fruit whose proliferation around the globe is closely connected to paths of European imperialism and colonialism.

Americans have historically been conservative in experimentation with tropical and subtropical fruits. Some tropical fruits native to Mexico and South America were slow to become popular in the United States. For example, the avocado was a staple food of the Aztecs and Mayans in Mexico and Central America long before any Europeans arrived. The name of this now familiar fruit is derived from the Aztec word for it, *ahuacatl*. But avocados weren't grown in the United States until 1833, when a prominent horticulturist began cultivating them in southern Florida. And although avocados had been grown for centuries in northern Mexico, they weren't planted in southern California until 1871. Other fruits indigenous to Central and South America still struggle in gaining acceptance in the U.S. market. Although guavas are one of the most popular fruits of Cuba, they remain exotic and unfamiliar to most Americans. Coconuts, indigenous to Southeast Asia, remain more familiar to us than many native fruits of the Americas, like cherimoya, cactus pears, mamey sapotes, and pepino melons.

American entrepreneurs began to see the enormous possibilities of tropical fruits in the late 1800s. Increasing popular demands for exotic fruits led some adventurous and risk-taking businessmen to explore their commercial potential. In 1870, Cape Cod skipper Lorenzo Dow Baker sailed his schooner, the *Telegraph,* to Port Morant, Jamaica, where he loaded it with bananas and coconuts. He then returned to New Jersey, where he sold his fruit cargo at a huge profit. In 1885, Baker established the Boston Fruit Company, and, fourteen years later, founded the United Fruit Company (UFC) in partnership with an American businessman named Minor Keith. The UFC was one of the first fruit-growing and -importing companies to gain considerable economic and political clout in Central America, exploiting local labor, prompting political factionalism, and fueling increasing unrest that would contribute to political and armed revolution in the mid-1900s.

On the other side of the Atlantic, Europeans were also gaining access to tropical fruits. In the 1870s, British fruit importer Thomas Fyffe found commercial success by controlling temperatures in his ships' holds to ensure preservation of tropical fruits during the ocean passage from the Canary Islands to England. Another Brit, Henry Arthur Stockley, is largely responsible for popularizing bananas in England. Because British wholesalers had no refrigerated facilities and were widely suspicious of Stockley's entrepreneurial activities with tropical fruits, Stockley sold directly to individual street peddlers, called costermongers. These peddlers sold exotic tropical fruits directly to consumers off their street carts, enabling people from all classes to enjoy this produce, which had previously only been available to the wealthiest citizens. While in the 1870s bananas had been an expensive and rare delicacy in England, one story recounts an incident in 1901 of a beggar becoming indignant when a clergyman gave him a banana. The beggar complained that he could buy a banana anywhere for half a cent, and then knocked the cleric down in contempt.

Another familiar tropical fruit that led the growth of importation was the pineapple. In the United States today, the brand name Dole is synonymous with Hawaiian pineapples. In 1903, Honolulu-born Harvard graduate James Drummond Dole began his business by exporting two thousand cases of canned pineapple. Pineapples, which had been introduced to Hawaii from the East Indies, were so plentiful and common on those islands that they cost only a penny apiece. By raising capital to establish a canning business, which he named the Hawaiian Pineapple Company, Dole turned this inexpensive Hawaiian fruit into a multimillion-dollar industry. Within a few years of start-up, his cannery was churning out two thousand cases in as little as fifteen minutes.

Tropical spices were integrated into European and American cuisines long before tropical fruits. Roman desires for spices to season and preserve their foods increased dramatically in the first century A.D. Before this time, Arabian merchants controlled the spice trade, transporting the valuable foodstuffs from Arabia and the Far East to the Roman Empire. In A.D. 90, Romans broke the Arab monopoly on the spice trade, bypassing Arabian middlemen by sailing their own ships from the Egyptian Red Sea to India. The Romans' passion for spices has been blamed as a leading factor in the empire's collapse, as their efforts to procure the precious seasonings drained their gold reserves. In Revelations 18:11–3, Christian prophet John of Ephesus complained of Roman excesses in the name of spices.

The Roman Empire collapsed in 476, and Constantinople ruled European lands and spice imports for almost 1,000 years. In 1473, Constantinople fell to the Muslim Ottoman Empire, which imposed unprecedented high import taxes on caravan shipments and spices. With guidance from Marco Polo's written records of his travels to China, Indonesia, and the Spice Islands (Moluccas) in the late 1200s, Portuguese traders sought to avoid Ottoman tariffs and undermine the expansion of Muslim political control by finding their own way to native lands of spices. They successfully sailed around southern Africa to India in the late 1400s. Arab merchants in India were not pleased to see the Portuguese arrive. One merchant cursed a Portuguese officer when he met him in the Calicut port: "The devil take you! What are you doing here?" "We have come in search of spices and Christians," replied the officer. This initial expedition for spices also gave the Portuguese a foothold in African coastal regions, leading to commercial exchanges with African kingdoms, the spread of Christian missionaries into Africa, and, eventually, the African slave trade that supported sugar production in the Caribbean.

No other foodstuffs have been at the center of so many wars and conflicts as tropical spices. Romans, Arabs, Ottomans, and Europeans battled with each other for control over these precious commodities—and the lands and indigenous populations where they grew—for nearly 1,800 years. The monopolies on spices weren't broken until 1788, when a small schooner from Salem, Massachusetts, snuck into the Dutch East Indies and brought a boatload of pepper, cassia, cinnamon, and camphor home to the United States. The Massachusetts skipper, Captain Carnes, surprised the world by finding the exact location of the Spice Islands that the Dutch had successfully kept hidden from the rest of the world for almost two hundred years. Spices attained widespread national commercial distribution in the United States in the early to mid-1900s, with the growth of McCormick Spices based out of Baltimore, Maryland, and the Spice Island Company based in San Francisco, California.

In the United States today, we often forget how privileged we are to have easy access to an enormous variety of tropical and subtropical products. We're accustomed to walking into our supermarkets and finding a wide range of produce from warmer climes. Imports of tropical and sub-tropical fruits are reaching all-time highs in the United States for a combination of reasons. These include increasing demand fueled by growing immigrant populations, expanding interests in international cuisine, and improved techniques and technology for preservation, packaging, and transport. Some of these fruits have long been familiar, like mounds of pink and yellow grapefruits larger than softballs or neatly stacked pyramids of brightly colored oranges, while others still seem exotic, foreign, and intimidating to our northern perspective.

What do you do with speckled orange and green papayas weighing as much as ten pounds, or football-shaped kiwano melons with daunting horns protruding from their spectacular orange rinds? What are lychees, longans, kumquats, and guavas, and how are their flavors best enjoyed? What kinds of nuts and spices best complement these exotic fruits? I hope the repertoire of following recipes answers these questions and many more, as they lead you to new understanding and appreciation of the wide range of tropical fruits, nuts, and spices we're so lucky to have available to us.

Tropical Desserts Glossary:
A Guide to the Fruits, Nuts, and Spices in these Recipes

FRUITS

Asian Pears

Also called apple pears or sand pears, Asian pears are indigenous to China and Japan, and are still grown extensively there. They are also cultivated in California and the western United States, where they were first introduced by Chinese miners during the California Gold Rush. Asian pears are round like apples, with skins ranging in color from brown to yellow to green, sometimes speckled or russeted. Their flesh is white and succulent with juice, and so crisp that they can be sliced very thinly, unlike other pears. Choose ones that are firm and fragrant smelling. Asian pears are great for baking because their juicy, firm flesh becomes sweet without losing its shape. They are in season in late summer and early fall.

Avocados

Avocados, or alligator pears, are native to Mexico, Central America, and South America, and are now cultivated in many subtropical regions around the world. The name derived from *ahuacatl,* the Aztec word for the fruit. In the United States, avocados are primarily produced in Florida and California. There are three main varieties available: Mexican, Guatemalan, and West Indian. The common

California Haas variety, frequently found in our supermarkets, is a commercial hybrid of the Guatemalan and Mexican. Florida avocados, which are a hybrid of Guatemalan and West Indian, are larger and smoother-skinned than the Haas.

Bananas

Bananas are one of the most prolific and well-known fruits of the world. Although native to Southeast Asia, they are now widely cultivated in most tropical countries. Baby bananas, also called niño, fig, or ladyfinger bananas, are a small, plump variety with very thin skins; they are generally sweeter and more flavorful than regular bananas. Red bananas are also smaller and plumper than regular ones, with deep maroon skins and white to pinkish flesh. Because of their strong, full flavor, red bananas are preferable to use whenever the fruit is called for. Choose bunches with fruit that appears plump and full; fruits that are thin and flat were probably picked too soon.

Cactus Pears

Cactus pears, also commonly called prickly pears, are the fruit of the opuntia or nopales desert cactus. Indigenous to the deserts of northwestern Mexico and southwestern United States, they are now grown in many other areas of the world, including Mediterranean countries, Australia, southern Africa, southwestern Asia, Central and South America. Varieties commonly sold in the United States have skins ranging in color from green to garnet red or purple. The bright red or pale green flesh has a flavor reminiscent of watermelons. Cactus pears' peak seasons are fall and winter; choose ones that are firm, thin-skinned, and have fewer spines.

Carambola

Carambola, or starfruit, is native to Java and Southeast Asia, and is now cultivated in Malaysia, Central and South America, the Caribbean, Hawaii, and, most recently, Florida. It earned its common nickname, star fruit, because of its five-pointed star shape when sliced crossways. The thin, yellow skin is edible, and the pale, translucent flesh ranges in flavor from sweetly fragrant to acidic and lemon-like. Carambola do not take very well to heat, as they shrivel and lose their juicy character. They are best enjoyed sliced raw to retain their crisp, refreshing acidic bite. Choose firm fruits with full ribs. Carambola are ripe and at their sweetest when bright yellow, but can be purchased green and allowed to ripen. They are generally available from August to March.

Cherimoya

Cherimoyas are indigenous to the high, mountainous areas of Peru and Ecuador, and may be the earliest recorded New World fruit. They are now grown in Australia, New Zealand, Spain, Israel, Mexico, Central America, Jamaica, and, most recently, California. The green rinds can be cone-shaped, heart-shaped, or roundish, either smooth or with depressions resembling fingerprints. The smooth, cream-colored flesh is juicy with a heavenly flavor resembling combinations of mango, papaya, pineapple, and vanilla. Be sure to remove the large, inedible black seeds. Choose ones that are uniformly green and avoid those with moldy or cracked flesh near the stem, indicating overripeness. Store at room temperature because refrigeration will deteriorate them. Cherimoyas are primarily available in winter months.

Cocoa

Cocoa is native to Mexico and Central America, and is now also commercially produced in South America, West Africa, and the West Indies. Cocoa beans form inside pods that grow from the trunks of cacao trees, and are extremely bitter before processing. Raw cocoa beans are roasted and then ground into a dark brown paste called chocolate liquor, which is then separated into dark cocoa powder and white cocoa butter, the central ingredient of white chocolate. In this book, I use chocolate as a supporting flavor to other tropical products. Its widely loved richness goes well with banana, coconut, caramel, coffee, orange and kumquat, cinnamon, allspice, clove, nutmeg, ginger, and any kind of tropical nut.

Coconuts

Coconuts are native to Southeast Asia but are now grown in many tropical coastal regions, including West Africa, South America, the Caribbean, South Pacific Islands, and parts of

India. The coconut palm reaches towering heights of one hundred feet. Although they don't begin to bear fruit until they are fifteen to twenty years old, mature trees can yield fifty to one hundred coconuts per year. When you crack open a coconut, save the "milk" enclosed inside, which actually resembles clouded water more than milk. You can drink the milk straight, enjoying its sweet, mild coconut flavor, or use it to flavor sauces, curries, desserts, or baked goods. Fresh coconuts are always worth the effort to crack open, as they are more moist and flavorful than dried coconut.

Coffee Beans

Coffee beans are the inner fruit of the bright red berries borne by the coffee plant, an evergreen shrub. Indigenous to the Ethiopian highlands of East Africa, coffee is now grown extensively in South America, Central America, West Indies, East Indies, and Arabia. The name is derived from the Arabian word *qahwah,* an infusion of the beans. The dried beans are greenish in color before they are roasted to create the dark, brown beans of varying shades with which we are familiar. Coffee has long been a popular dessert ingredient.

Dates

Dates are the fruit of the date palm, indigenous to the Middle East and also grown in North Africa, Arizona, and California. Date palms were an ancient source of natural wealth in Persian, Arabian, Mesopotamian, and North African societies, because every part of the wood, leaves, sap, and fruit was used for a wide range of human needs. Dates have paper-thin skins and intensely sweet, sticky flesh. They are yellow, golden, or black when fresh, but are most commonly found in the United States in dried or semidried form, brown in color.

Feijoa

Feijoa, also called pineapple guava, are native to South America and now commercially produced in New Zealand. Related to guavas, they belong to the Myrtle family, which also includes cloves, allspice, and eucalyptus. Feijoa were introduced to California as early as 1900. Because they can be easier to find in the United States than guavas, you can use them as a substitute for guavas in any of these recipes. Feijoa are a fragrant and slightly tart fruit with a complex flavor suggesting combinations of quince, pineapple, spruce, and Concord grapes. This long, oval fruit has bright green skin that is often bumpy, like avocado skin, and flesh that ranges from off-white to pale yellow. Feijoas imported from New Zealand are usually available in spring and early summer, while the California season is from fall to early winter.

Figs

Figs are native to the Middle East and Mediterranean regions, where they symbolized peace and prosperity. Figs are now cultivated in California and the southern United States. Fresh figs can be colored white, green, purple, or black, and can be either onion-shaped or pear-shaped. The flesh ranges from white to red, with a soft texture and slightly nutty flavor. Figs have one of the highest contents of natural sugar, sometimes exceeding 62 percent. They are available periodically through spring, summer, or fall.

Grapefruits

Grapefruits are indigenous to Jamaica, but have become a quintessential American fruit, produced extensively in Florida, California, Texas, and Arizona. Grapefruits earned their name because they grow in bunches, like grapes. They can have either thick or thin skins ranging in color from yellow to pink, with white, yellow, pink, or ruby red colored flesh. Although popularized as a breakfast fruit, their bittersweet flavor and thirst-quenching quality is enjoyable at any time of day. Pink and yellow grapefruits are available year-round, while the ruby red variety, produced primarily in Texas, is in season from fall to winter.

Guavas

Guavas are native to Brazil, and are now cultivated in South America, Central America, the Caribbean, Mexico, Hawaii, Australia, India, and South Africa. Most of the guavas available in our supermarkets are produced in Florida. Guavas can be either roundish or pear-shaped, with skin that may be yellow, green, or pink. Flavors vary according to the variety, and may be reminiscent of combinations of pineapple, banana, lemon, or strawberry. The white, pink, or yellow flesh is meaty and has small, edible seeds. When fully ripe, guavas are fragrantly aromatic and smell distinctly like bubble gum. Although guava paste or jelly can usually be found in Hispanic specialty stores,

I only like to use fresh guavas, pureed for sorbets or custards, or paired with other tropical fruits.

Key Limes

Key limes, also called Mexican or West Indian limes, are the most flavorful variety of this tart citrus. Produced extensively in the Florida Keys, Mexico, and the Caribbean, they are originally from India and Asia. Key limes have thin, yellow-green skins, and tart, yellow flesh. They have a very high vitamin C content; the nickname "limey" for seamen dates from the 18th century, when British sailors consumed key limes to prevent scurvy. If you can't find key limes, you can replace them with the smaller, dark green limes commonly found in stores, at a ratio of 1 1/2 regular limes to 1 key lime.

Kiwano Melons

Kiwano melons, native to Africa, are also produced in California and New Zealand. They were a very important fruit for hunting and gathering societies in southern Africa. Also called horned melons, they have a very striking appearance with bright orange-yellow skin covered with dull spikes. The green flesh has a jellyish texture that tastes like a cross between watermelon, banana, and cucumber. Because they have so many seeds, kiwanos should be processed by pureeing and straining the flesh.

Kiwi

Kiwi fruits are native to China and are also called Chinese gooseberries. New Zealand began cultivating subtropical kiwis in the early 19th century and is now the largest commercial producer, although they're also grown in California, Europe, South Africa, and India. The name was changed from Chinese gooseberry to kiwi in the 1950s, as a marketing tactic to overcome anti-Communist fears of anything identified as Chinese. In the 1970s and 1980s, kiwis became a favored, and overused, fruit of nouvelle cuisine. The fruit is about the size of a large egg, with furry light brown skin, green flesh, and edible black seeds. Kiwis have a distinctive tart "green" flavor.

Kumquats

Kumquats are native to China, and the name is Cantonese for "golden orange." They are also commercially produced in Japan, Florida, and California. Kumquats are unique in that their rind is fragrantly sweet while the inner pulp is bitter and acidic. Their are two main varieties, each about 1 1/2 inches long: the Meiwa, which is roundish and slightly sweeter, and the Nagami, generally more oval in shape. I like to process kumquats by first boiling them in water to extract bitterness, then candying them in a simple sugar syrup. They are primarily available in winter months.

Lemons

Lemons are probably native to northern India or Malaysia, from whence they spread to Assyria and Mediterranean countries. Lemons are now commercially produced in California and Spain and cultivated, to a lesser extent, in many subtropical regions around the world. Although we're familiar with lemons when they've ripened to a canary yellow color, they are usually picked when green and then "cured" in a temperature-controlled environment. Lemon skins may be either thick or thin, and the tart flesh and juice are high in vitamin C.

Lemon Grass

Lemon grass, native to Malaysia, is related to citronella grasses, which are used in many insect repellents. It's cultivated in many parts of the world, including West Africa, Southeast Asia, Australia, Central America, Florida, and California. Lemon grass has stiff, gray-green stalks and coarse, strawlike upper grasses. Inside the stalk is a light-colored tender core similar to a scallion bulb, which can be used to add bright lemon flavor to dishes. Lemon grass is generally available year-round, in some supermarkets and natural food stores or in Asian specialty stores.

Longans

Longans are native to Southeast Asia and China, and are also grown in India and southern Florida, where they were first introduced by an American missionary living in China. They are related to the lychee (see below), though slightly more hardy. The fruits, which are generally about the size of a large olive, grow in small clusters on large shade trees with dark green leaves. Longans have leathery brown skins that can be easily removed, juicy gray-white flesh, and an inedible black pit. Their flavor is reminiscent of spice, musk, and hints of floral gardenia. Longans can generally be found in Asian specialty stores during summer months.

Lychees

Lychees are one of the most popular Chinese fruits, and have been cultivated there for more than two thousand years. They're also now grown in Southeast Asia, India, South Africa, Australia, Mexico, and Hawaii. Lychees are strawberry-like in appearance, with leathery skin ranging in color from pink to garnet red to brown, juicy white flesh that is easily removed, and an inedible brown seed. They are available fresh in summer months, and will store in the refrigerator for several weeks. They're also available dried (lychee "nuts"), with a very different chewy and smoky flavor, or canned in syrup.

Mamey Sapote

Mamey sapotes are native to Central America and also widely cultivated in South America, Mexico, and the Caribbean. Their trees are related to sapodilla trees, from which chicle is harvested to make chewing gum. Their skin is a bit rough and fuzzy, ranging in color from brown to red, and the salmon-colored or orange-red flesh tastes like a cross between sweet potato, avocado, and honey. Look for these large, oval fruits in the summer months. Mameys are wonderful fruits to feature a central flavor in desserts, as their rich and creamy flavor naturally lends itself to dessert-making. They make excellent soups, sorbets, or ice creams, or simply cut them fresh and serve them with an assortment of other tropical fruits.

Mangoes

Mangoes are native to India and Southeast Asia, where they have been grown for at least six thousand years, and are now widely cultivated in many tropical and subtropical regions around the world. Many of the mangoes we see in our supermarkets are produced in Florida, Mexico, Haiti, or the Caribbean. Most fruits are kidney shaped, though some are round, with smooth skins ranging in color from green to mottled red to orange-red. The perfumed, aromatic orange flesh must be cut away from the large inner pit with a sharp knife. If not yet ripe, the flesh will be fibrous and hard; the pit may also be covered with fibers of varying length. Domestic mangoes are available in the summer, while imported ones are often available in winter.

Oranges

Oranges, which are probably native to southern China and Southeast Asia, can be divided into two main varieties: sweet and sour. Sweet oranges, the ones we are most familiar with, are now staple crops of California and Florida in the United States. Blood oranges are a type of sweet orange that have a beautiful, striking appearance. Their flesh may be orange with garnet red tones, or may be entirely scarlet in color. Tangerines or mandarins are another type of sweet orange, smaller with somewhat flattened tops and bottoms. Their skins may be either thick or thin, and are usually easy to peel. The medium-sized, seedless Satsuma mandarins are especially sweet, aromatic, and flavorful. Bitter oranges, also known as sour oranges or Seville oranges, are thought to be the ancestors of all varieties of this fruit. They are too acidic to be eaten raw, but are used for a wide variety of cooking purposes. Despite their name, many oranges remain green even when ripe, so don't be deterred by fruits that may have green or yellow tones to them—they may be sweeter and juicier than the orangest ones!

Papayas

Papayas, also called pawpaws or papaws, are native to tropical America and are now widely cultivated in many tropical regions of the world. Many of our papayas are produced in Hawaii. Don't confuse tropical pawpaws (papayas) with the indigenous wild North American pawpaws, which resemble thick, dark brown bananas. Papayas grow in clusters on large, single-stemmed trees, resembling the coconut palm in form but shorter and with different-shaped leaves. Papaya contains an enzyme called "papain," which is aids in digestion and is also used as a meat tenderizer and deep cleanser. The ones we see in our stores are generally small in scale, similar in size to mangoes, but they can grow extremely large, up to twenty pounds. The smooth skin ranges in color from green to orange-gold, and the aromatic flesh can be yellow, orange, or rose-colored. They are generally available year-round.

Passion Fruit

Passion fruits are native to Brazil, and are now cultivated in the South Pacific, Central America, Africa, India, Taiwan, Hawaii, Florida, and California. They are the fruit of a vine that also produces striking flowers from which the fruit earned its name: the flowers are said to resemble the Passion of Christ at his crucifixion, with its different parts representing his wounds, crucifixion nails, crown of thorns, and surrounding Apostles. The fruits are roundish and small, with thick, tough, bumpy skin and yellowish pulp and seeds inside. Most skins are colored rusty red or dark purple with brown tones, though yellow ones are produced on a lesser scale. They are available year-round. Passion fruits are a "delicacy" among tropical fruits, with a clean, zesty, and citrusy flavor. The seedy pulp should always be pulsed in a blender a few times to separate the seeds from the flesh, then passed through a fine strainer. The resulting "juice" is extremely tart and potent.

Pepino Melons

Pepino melons, which are also called melon pears or, my favorite, mellowfruit, are native to the South American Andes regions and are now produced extensively in New Zealand. Pepinos have become extremely popular in Japan, where people give them as gifts and use them ornamentally as well as for desserts. Pepino means "cucumber" in Spanish, and the golden yellow flesh has flavors reminiscent of this vegetable. The rind is also yellow, attractively adorned with purple stripes. Choose melons which are sweetly fragrant and free of bruises, with golden to apricot-colored skins. They are generally in season in winter and spring.

Persimmons

Persimmons are of two main types: Japanese persimmons, native to China but primarily produced in Japan, and the smaller, native eastern American persimmons, which were an important part of the Algonquin diet. The Japanese varieties are called for in this book, and are commonly available in stores. They're now widely grown in California, Europe, North Africa, and Chile. They have smooth, orange skin and flesh of the same color that is reminiscent of plums, pumpkins, and honey. Choose ones that are very soft with a deep, orange color. If not fully ripe, they will be bitter and tannic. Specialty-produce expert Elizabeth Schneider recommends ripening too-firm persimmons by enclosing them in a bag with an apple or a banana, or in an airtight plastic container with a few drops of rum, bourbon, or other liquor on the tops of the stems, and letting them sit for three to six days. Persimmons are generally available in late fall and winter.

Pineapples

Pineapples, one of America's favorite tropical fruits, are indigenous to Central and South America and are now widely grown in most tropical regions. They were named for their pinecone-like appearance, and are produced by a low, spreading, cactuslike plant. Botanically, the pineapple is composed of many individual multiple fruits: those diamond, hexagonal shapes that form the rough and bumpy skin. The flesh is yellow or white, and should be very juicy when ripe. Choose fruits that have golden and yellow skin tones, rather than green ones. Ripeness of some varieties can be determined by plucking out one of the leaves; if it can be easily removed, it's ready to eat!

Plantains

Plantains, also commonly called cooking bananas, are native to Southeast Asia and are now grown throughout the tropics. They are starchier than bananas and are often used in savory dishes, prepared like potatoes into a mash, fried as chips or fritters, or cooked in stews. Although we prefer that the starchy flesh is cooked, they are eaten raw in some tropical regions. Plantains can be used at different stages of ripeness, from green to bright yellow to brown and black. The blacker the skin, the riper and softer the flesh. Plantains keep for a considerable period of time, even when black and fully ripe. Green plantains are great for frying into chips. Fully ripe plantains have a strong banana flavor.

Pomegranates

Pomegranates, though the size of apples or oranges, are actually a member of the berry family. Probably native to Persia, they've long been an important fruit in many Middle Eastern, Near Eastern, and Mediterranean societies. Although there are many varieties, the one primarily available in the United States is called "Wonderful" or "Red Wonderful," with a reddish-brown, leathery shell and scarlet-colored large seeds inside. Only the seeds, which are sweet and tart, are edible. Grenadine syrup is made from pomegranate seeds, and derives its name from the French word for the fruit, *grenade.* Choose pomegranates that are heavy, large, and deeply colored. Be careful when handling, for the juice will stain your clothes indelibly! Their prime season is in late fall and early winter.

Tamarillos

Tamarillos are native to the South American Andes regions, and are now grown throughout South and Central America, the Caribbean, South Pacific, and to a limited extent in California. Related to eggplants, the fruits are aesthetically beautiful with glossy, smooth skins colored golden or red and apricot-colored flesh with purple seeds. The bitter skin must be peeled but the bittersweet flesh can be used in savory dishes, or, when sweetened with sugar, in desserts. Choose unblemished, firm, heavier fruits. They make a fantastic acidic sorbet that can balance out many of the sweeter tropical fruits, like papayas or mangoes. Tamarillos are generally available from early summer through fall.

Tamarind

Tamarind is native to India and produced throughout Southeast Asia, Africa, and Mexico. They are long, brown pods grown on large, spreading trees that can reach eighty feet. Inside the pods are tamarind seeds and a sticky, brown pulp with both sweet and tart tones.

Tomatillos

Tomatillos, also called Chinese lantern plants or Mexican green tomatoes, are actually related to gooseberries. They're native to Mexico, and were a delicacy in ancient Aztec civilization. Today, their production remains oddly limited to Mexico and the southwestern United States. They are most commonly apple-green colored, with darker green paper husks surrounding them. Choose ones that are firm and dry with close-fitting husks. Tomatillos are generally available year-round. Their tart flavor is unique for its light, refreshing quality.

NUTS

Almonds

Almonds are the kernels of a leathery fruit produced by the almond tree. Native to the Near East, they are now grown extensively for commercial purposes in California, Australia, and South Africa. Sweet almonds are the variety with which we are most familiar; bitter almonds are primarily pressed for almond oil. Almonds are a popular snack food, and are widely used for sweet pastries, confections, and cakes. California crops generally ripen in the late summer months of August and September, and are processed and ready for shipment by November.

Brazil Nuts

Brazil nuts, as their name suggests, are native to South America, and flourish in the Amazonian regions of Brazil, Peru, and Bolivia. The nuts grow inside large, round, hard castaña pods on gigantic castaña trees that can reach 130 feet or more, with their lowest branches one hundred feet above the ground. Individual Brazil nuts are encased inside wrinkled, dark brown, triangular-shaped shells that are very difficult to crack. Surprisingly, Brazil nuts are much cheaper than many other precious nuts, like piñons or cashews, and have become increasingly available in the United States, as they've become an important commodity for sustainable development and eco-enterprise projects in threatened rain forest regions.

Cashews

Cashews are costly but delicious kidney-shaped nuts that are products of large, spreading savanna trees, and are widely cultivated in tropical savanna regions. The nuts grow on the ends of pear-shaped, juicy cashew fruits, which range in color from yellow to pinkish-red and have a unique, subtle sweet flavor reminiscent of crisp apples and grapes. The nuts are commonly available either raw or roasted, whole or broken. They have a rich, buttery flavor with slightly floral tones.

Macadamias

Macadamias are indigenous to Australia, and were named after John Macadam, a Scottish-born Australian chemist who cultivated the nuts. Hawaii now produces them extensively for commercial purposes, and, to a lesser extent, so does California. The white nuts are covered by a hard, brown shell that is encased in smooth, green husks. They grow in clusters on evergreen trees, and although the green husks naturally split open when ripe, the brown shells are difficult to crack. Macadamias are rich with buttery flavor tones, and are available either raw or roasted.

Peanuts

Peanuts, also called groundnuts, grow in their familiar brown shells beneath the ground. They are widely cultivated in many tropical and subtropical regions, including Africa, parts of the Far East, Indonesia, and the southern United States. The peanut is a favorite American nut, especially in the form of peanut butter or eaten as a snack food. Many other cultures use peanuts for a wider range of savory uses, such as West African peanut stews or Thai peanut sauces. It is interesting to note that peanut shells are often burned as fuel and their ashes used as fertilizer, or can be ground into a meal that is used in metal polishes by steel mills.

Pecans

Pecans are nuts of a hickory tree indigenous to Mississippi valley regions and river valleys in parts of Texas, and now grown throughout the southern United States, Mexico, and parts of South America. Commercial production of pecans has been relatively limited, making them a precious nut with a higher price range.

Pistachios

Pistachios are the kernels of the small, reddish fruit of trees bearing the same name. Native to western Asia, they are now widely cultivated throughout Mediterranean countries and some in California. The oval nut, which has a thin brown shell and meat ranging in color from light green to yellow, has a delicate, sweet flavor. Don't be fooled by red pistachios, which are artificially colored with red dye for commercial marketing reasons. Buy unsalted brown ones for baking or use in desserts or ice creams.

Piñons

Piñons, also called pine nuts or pignolias, are seeds of the piñon tree, which grows in subtropical climates around the world, including China, Italy, southern France, Spain, southwestern United States, Mexico, and parts of South

America. They are widely used in Mediterranean, South-western, and Native American cuisines, for both savory and sweet dishes. Piñons can be bland when raw but have a delicious, distinctive flavor when roasted.

SPICES

Allspice

Allspice, also called Jamaican pepper, is a small, round dried fruit of an evergreen tree native to the Caribbean and coastal areas of Central America. Nearly two-thirds of the allspice imported to the United States is produced in Jamaica. It is commonly available in ground, powdered form, but can also be purchased in whole form. It earned its name because its pungent fragrance resembles a combination of cinnamon, nutmeg, and cloves.

Aniseed

Aniseed is the dried fruit of anise, a lightly licorice-flavored herbaceous plant related to parsley and carrot. Native to Egypt, it is now widely cultivated in many subtropical regions. Most of the aniseed imported to the United States comes from Turkey, Spain, and Syria. Its mild, licorice taste is often used to flavor cakes, cookies, and candies. Its refreshing tones can enliven many preparations that are otherwise unexciting.

Cardamom

Cardamom is the dried fruit of an herbaceous plant that is related to ginger. It is native to India, and is also cultivated in Ceylon and Central America. Cardamom can be purchased either in whole, seed form or in ground, powdered form. Its warm, pungent aroma is widely used in Indian cooking and is a central ingredient to curries. In the Middle East, coffee is flavored with cardamom. It's excellent for flavoring breads, cakes, cookies, custards, and puddings.

Cinnamon

Cinnamon is the dried inner bark of a family of evergreen trees. Different species of trees in Ceylon, China, southeast Asia, and Indonesia produce slightly different forms of this spice. Cinnamon is a staple spice of most American kitchens, widely used for baking, pastries, candies, and pickling. It can be purchased ground or in whole "stick" form, which is actually a piece of dried, curled bark. Cinnamon is perhaps the quintessential spice, a fantastic complement to most fruits and a familiar earthy rich flavor that everyone loves. Canela is a type of Mexican cinnamon that is sweeter and usually more fragrant than other forms from the East, and is often my first choice for dessert-making.

Cloves

Cloves are dried flower buds of an evergreen tree native to the Moluccas or Spice Islands in Indonesia. It is also cultivated in Madagascar, the Zanzibar and Pemba islands off the coast of Tanzania, Malaysia, and India. The word clove is derived from the Latin clavus, meaning "nail," which the dried buds resemble in shape. It can be purchased in either ground or whole form. Take caution when handling whole cloves to avoid knocking the flavorful "crown" off the stem. Cloves are powerful and pungent, and must be used in desserts with a light touch. Citrus fruits hold up particularly well to the strong character of cloves, but try them with a variety of other, sweeter tropical fruits as well.

Ginger

Ginger is the root of an herbaceous plant believed to be native to Southeast Asia or Africa, and is also cultivated in Jamaica, India, Indonesia, China, and Japan. Ginger roots, which range from 2 1/2 to 4 inches in length, are sometimes called "hands" because of their fingerlike extrusions. Its pungent, refreshing flavor is valued in many cuisines and cultures, from Japanese sushi to African stews. Fresh ginger can be found in most produce sections of supermarkets, and should be peeled before use. Dried, ground ginger is widely used for spicing cakes and cookies, including familiar gingerbread and ginger snaps.

Nutmeg and Mace

Nutmeg and mace are both products of the same evergreen tree native to the Moluccas or Spice Islands in Indonesia, now cultivated in many tropical and subtropical regions of the world. Nutmeg is the seed of the tree while mace is the aril, or exterior covering, of the seed. The mace is removed from the nutmeg after harvesting, and the two spices are dried separately. Nutmegs are available either whole or ground, and are commonly used to flavor pies, puddings, and some beverages, such as eggnog. Mace is available whole, broken, or ground. Its fragrant, mild, nutmeglike flavor is also used in baking, and is widely used by commercial manufacturers of relishes, sauces, and canned meats.

Pepper

Pepper is the dried berry of a vine indigenous to the Malabar coast of southern India, and is now cultivated in many tropical and subtropical regions, including Malaysia, Indonesia, and Brazil. Black peppercorns are made by boiling the berries in water and then laying them out in the sun to dry as quickly as possible. White peppercorns are made by drying the berries more slowly, keeping them in moist heaps or soaking them in water for several days before laying them in the sun for a day or two. Pepper is a familiar tabletop spice in the United States, liberally used for seasoning a wide variety of dishes. Although not normally considered a dessert spice, finely ground pepper is excellent for seasoning fruits, particularly papaya and figs.

Sesame Seeds

Sesame seeds are products of an herbaceous plant native to Asia and widely grown in East Africa, the Near East, West Indies, and Central America. We are most familiar with hulled sesame seeds, which are cream colored. Unhulled seeds range in color from yellowish-white to black, with shades of brown in between. The pleasant, nutty flavor of sesame is widely used for breads, cookies, and sweet honey pastries. In the Middle East, they are finely ground with almonds and sugar to make halvah, a popular confection.

Star Anise

Star anise is the dried fruit of a shrub that is native to the Far East. It earned its name because it's shaped like an eight-pointed star, with a diameter ranging from 1/2 to 1 inch wide. The British first imported star anise to Europe during the Renaissance, where it is commonly used in infusions and liqueurs, including anisette. Star anise has a slightly hot, aromatic aniseed flavor.

Vanilla Beans

Vanilla beans are the seed pods of an orchid plant indigenous to tropical regions of Central and South America. The string beanlike pods are soaked in alcohol in order to make vanilla extract, a common baking seasoning in American kitchens. Whole vanilla beans have an especially intense, vanilla flavor, and can be purchased in specialty or natural-food stores. Vanilla beans can be infused into custards, syrups, and poaching liquids for fruits. After infusing them once, the beans still contain a lot of vanilla flavor. You can soak them in vodka to make your own extract, or dry them and place them in a jar of granulated sugar to make some delicious vanilla-scented sugar.

Cold Desserts

The warmth and heat of the tropics provide natural inspiration for creating frozen or cold desserts from abundant tropical products. Many of the following recipes would be most refreshing during warmer months of the year because of their chilled nature. What could be more invigorating than Key Lime Granita on a sultry summer afternoon, or more decadent than a Pineapple-Coconut Ice Cream Float after returning from the beach? But we all know that colder climates don't deter us from indulging in one of our favorite frozen desserts, ice cream, so these recipes are by no means limited to warm weather. Heat up a chilly winter night with Chinese Five-Spice Ice Cream, or serve the aromatic Grapefruit-Clove Sorbet after a holiday meal.

Several different forms of frozen desserts are included among these recipes: granitas, ice creams, sorbets, cassatas, bombes, and floats. The first known description of a frozen dessert dates from the 4th century B.C., when cooks in the court of Alexander the Great froze chopped fruit by placing it in earthenware jars surrounded by snow. In the 13th century A.D., the Chinese invented a process for freezing fruit mixtures by immersing pottery jars in cold water and saltpeter. Marco Polo learned this technique during his travels in China and introduced it to Europeans when he returned home. By the 17th century, frozen desserts were being enjoyed throughout Europe, but the English first invented ice cream as we know it today. In the 19th century, Auguste Escoffier refined techniques for making ice cream by basing the recipes on a crème anglaise custard. For the ice cream and sorbet recipes in this chapter, you will need an ice cream machine to spin the custards into solid frozen desserts. If you don't have an ice cream machine, you can still make the granitas, simple forms of ices that are frozen in pans.

Most of these cold desserts can be made in advance and refrigerated or frozen until serving. Ice creams and sorbets will keep in the freezer for several days, and can be brought out twenty minutes before serving to allow time for softening.

Cakes, tortes, or tarts can be prepared a day ahead of time, and their final assembly finished in the last minutes before serving. When stored covered in the refrigerator for a day, the flavors will mingle, intersperse, and intensify. Puddings, custards, and crème brûlées can also be prepared in advance and chilled in the refrigerator, and their fruit or caramelized toppings finished just before serving.

Cold desserts make delicious and refreshing departures from hot or spicy meals. A cold dessert after a spicy entrée or hot dinner can be a satisfying and enjoyable ending. Chilled soups and cold compotes are an elegant way to serve tropical fruits and spices for special gatherings. A Mamey Sapote Soup with Carambola and Tangerine will certainly impress your guests and is sure to stimulate interesting conversation, especially when you tell them mamey sapotes are considered aphrodisiacs in some parts of the world! Cold tarts, puddings, and cakes are familiar forms of treats that seem transformed when studded with unusual fruits and nuts and flavored with tropical spices. Break some rules and explore new taste sensations by playing with tropical ingredients—bake avocados in a tart, jazz up a vanilla pudding with papaya, use tomatillos for sorbet instead of salsa, and make a banana split with a red banana!

Papaya-Ginger Soup with Kiwi Granita

Papaya-Ginger Soup with Kiwi Granita

*MAKES **8** SERVINGS*

Cool, refreshing fruit soups are always one of my favorite summer desserts. They are simple to make and an elegant choice for easy entertaining. In this soup, the hot bite of ginger balances out the sweetness of papaya. Although not necessary, I recommend serving it with a kiwi granita (recipe included) because the sharp, sour flavor of kiwi is a good match for smooth papaya. You can also replace the kiwi granita with any flavor sorbet or ice cream of your choice.

For the soup

1/4 cup finely minced gingerroot

1 1/4 cups water

1 Jamaican red papaya or other papaya

2 tablespoons lime juice

1 cup orange juice

1/8 teaspoon salt

1/8 cup honey

For the kiwi granita

8 kiwis

1/4 cup water

1/2 cup sugar

1 kiwi, peeled and sliced for garnish

To make the soup, in a saucepan, combine the fresh minced ginger with the water and bring to a simmer over medium heat. Reduce heat to low and simmer for 10 minutes.

Peel the papaya, slice in half lengthwise and scoop out the black seeds. Roughly chop the fruit and place in a blender. Add the lime juice, orange juice, salt, and honey to the blender. When the ginger has finished simmering, add to the blender and puree the mixture for 30 seconds. Strain through a fine strainer, transfer to a bowl or container, cover, and chill in the refrigerator.

To make the kiwi granita, peel the kiwis and remove the hard stem piece on the ends of each. Roughly chop and place in the blender with the 1/4 cup of water and sugar. Pulse the blender on and off for 30 seconds, so as not to break up the tiny black seeds that can turn the mixture bitter.

Pour the blended kiwi mixture into a pan, approximately 10×10×2 inches, cover and place in the freezer for 2 1/2 hours or overnight. Remove from the freezer and scrape the granita with a spoon, shaving the frozen mixture into a fluffy ice.

Scoop the granita with an ice cream scoop into the center of 8 chilled bowls. Pour approximately 1/2 cup of the papaya soup around the granita. Garnish with slices of papaya, if desired.

> *Both pepper and ginger grow wild in their respective countries, and yet here we buy them by weight—just as if they were so much gold and silver.*
> —PLINY THE ELDER

Mamey Sapote Soup with Carambola and Tangerine

The reddish-colored flesh of mamey sapote makes a beautiful, striking soup. Because the fruit is available in the summer season, this dish would be an excellent choice for an easy, light summer brunch dessert. (Some cultures consider mamey sapote to be an aphrodisiac, so you may want to save it for a romantic rendezvous!) Small tangerine sections sprinkled in the soup add a pleasant citrus element to the smooth honey-like flavor of mamey sapote, while slices of carambola add a succulent crunch.

1 mamey sapote

2 1/2 cups water

Juice of 1 lemon

1/2 cup sugar

1 teaspoon vanilla extract

1/2 teaspoon salt

1 or 2 carambola (starfruit)

2 or 3 tangerines

Peel the mamey sapote, cut in half, and remove the black pit. Roughly chop the fruit into 1-inch chunks. In a saucepan, combine half of the mamey sapote with the water, lemon juice, sugar, vanilla, and salt. Bring to a simmer over medium heat and simmer for 5 minutes. Remove from heat, pass through a fine strainer, and cool the mixture by placing in the refrigerator for 15 minutes.

Slice the carambola crossways into thin slices. Section the tangerines and peel off any white pith that may cling to the sections. Divide the chilled soup among 8 to 10 bowls. Sprinkle chunks of mamey sapote, slices of carambola, and sections of tangerine in each bowl and serve.

Vanilla Poached Tropical Fruit Compote

Compotes are a simple way to use several different fruits in one dish, showcasing the bounty of tropical produce. Adapt this recipe by changing the fruit varieties or limiting the number of fruits. Serve with sorbet or ice cream.

1 mango

1 papaya

1 banana

1 small pineapple

1 guava

1 cup orange juice

1/2 cup coconut water, drained from a fresh coconut

1 vanilla bean, split and scraped

1 cup coconut shavings, shaved with a peeler and roasted at 350°F for 12 to 14 minutes or until toasted brown

Using a sharp paring knife, peel the mango, cut the flesh from the pit and cut into angular 1- to 2-inch pieces. Peel the papaya, cut in half lengthwise, scoop out the seeds, and cut into angular 1- to 2-inch pieces. Peel the banana, slice in half lengthwise, and cut into angular 1- to 2-inch pieces. Trim the top and bottom off the pineapple and then slice off the skin, working around the fruit until finished. If the pineapple is large, use only half. Quarter the pineapple by cutting lengthwise from top to bottom. Trim the core from each quarter and cut the fruit into angular 1- to 2-inch pieces. Peel the guava and roughly chop the fruit into pieces.

Put the guava in a blender with the orange juice and coconut water and puree for 30 seconds, or until smooth. Pass the mixture through a fine strainer into a large saucepan. Add the vanilla bean to the pan and place over medium heat. When the mixture simmers, add the prepared fruits. Return to a simmer, stirring occasionally, for 2 minutes. Place the fruit in a large bowl and chill in the refrigerator at least 20 minutes.

Divide among 6 to 8 bowls, sprinkle with the coconut, and serve.

MAKES *6* TO *8* SERVINGS

This fruit salad is different than a compote because the fruit is not heated or cooked but is tossed in a lightly simmered "dressing" of ginger, brown sugar, orange juice, and balsamic vinegar. Crispy spring-roll wrappers can be bought packaged in Asian groceries and some natural food stores, and the spring-roll cups can be made well in advance. This dish may be served as an appetizer or as a dessert. If desired for dessert, it can be enhanced by a tropical sorbet or ice cream, like the Pineapple Sorbet (page 10) or Coconut Ice Cream (page 18).

2 blood oranges

1 mango

2 passion fruit

2 carambola (starfruit)

1 pineapple

1 teaspoon finely grated gingerroot

2 tablespoons brown sugar

1 teaspoon balsamic vinegar

2 tablespoons orange juice

1 package crispy spring-roll wrappers, in 8- to 10-inch-diameter squares

1 tablespoon powdered sugar

Using a sharp chef's knife, trim the tops and bottoms off the blood oranges, then cut all the peel and pith from the inner flesh, working your way around the fruit. Section the oranges by cutting between each membrane and removing each tender wedge of fruit. Using a sharp paring knife, peel the mango and trim the flesh from the pit. Cut the mango fruit into approximate 2-inch wedge-shaped pieces. Cut the carambola crossways into 1/8-inch-thick slices. Trim the top and bottom from the pineapple, then slice all the outer skin from the flesh, working your way around the fruit. Quarter the pineapple fruit lengthwise, trim the core from each quarter, and cut into 2-inch wedge-shaped pieces. Combine all the cut fruit in a large bowl.

Combine the grated ginger, brown sugar, balsamic vinegar, and orange juice in a saucepan and cook over medium heat for 2 to 3 minutes, stirring periodically. Pour the ginger mixture over the cut fruit and toss until the fruit is well coated. Place in the refrigerator to chill.

While the fruit is chilling, make the spring-roll cups. Brush the spring-roll wrappers with a pastry brush soaked in water. Preheat oven to 350°F. Brush a large muffin pan with oil or melted butter. Fit each circle into the cavities of the muffin pan so that the edges stick up in a decorative free-form fashion. Bake the cups in the oven for 12 to 14 minutes, or until golden brown. Dust the 6 to 8 spring-roll cups with powdered sugar. Remove them from the muffin pan while still warm and set aside until final assembly.

Place the cups on individual plates and fill with fruit. Serve.

Lychee Granita with Caramelized Bananas

MAKES **8** TO **10** SERVINGS

A granita is a flavored frozen ice that was invented in Italy in the 19th century. A semifrozen preparation with a more granular texture than sorbets, granitas are the predecessors of flavored Italian Ices that have become popular, refreshing summer treats in the United States. They are easy to make because no ice cream machine is needed. Lychees are a favorite Chinese fruit. Their aromatic flavor, reminiscent of muscat grapes, provides a clean, crisp ending to a meal and pairs very nicely with rich, caramelized bananas.

For the granita

18 to 22 lychees

1 cup water

Juice of 2 lemons

1/4 cup sugar

Dash of salt

For the caramelized bananas

1/2 cup sugar

4 bananas, peeled and diagonally sliced 1/8 inch thick

2 tablespoons brandy or rum (optional)

1/4 cup water

1 teaspoon vanilla extract

1/2 teaspoon ground cinnamon

To make the granita, working over a bowl, squeeze the lychee flesh from the pink leathery skins. Cut a slit the length of each fruit and squeeze out the pits. Place the lychee flesh and reserved juice in a blender with the water, lemon juice, sugar, and salt. Puree for 30 seconds. Pour the mixture into a 10-inch square pan with 2-inch-high sides. Cover and place in the freezer for at least 2 1/2 hours or overnight.

To prepare the bananas, sprinkle the sugar into a sauté pan and place over medium heat. Allow sugar to melt and begin to brown. When it begins to lightly smoke and is completely melted and browned, carefully add the banana slices and cook, stirring, for 1 minute. Add the brandy, water, and vanilla and continue to cook, so that the liquid reduces and melts the caramel to make a loose sauce. Remove from heat.

Spoon the banana slices among 8 to 10 bowls and sprinkle with cinnamon. Using the edge of a spoon, scrape shavings off the frozen granita to create a fluffy ice. Make a large scoop of granita and place on top of the banana servings. If desired, you may pack the granita into timbale-shaped molds and unmold the timbales on top of the bananas. Serve immediately.

Pomegranate Granita with Caramelized Grapefruit

*MAKES **8** TO **10** SERVINGS*

When I first tried a pomegranate as a teenager, I was bewildered about how to eat it. After being tipped off by a friend that the red seeds inside this funny fruit were the only edible part, my fingers quickly became stained pink as I dug the seeds out of the white membrane and enjoyed their tart, tangy flavor. Pomegranates make excellent, refreshing iced desserts, but you will need a food mill to crush the juice out of the seeds. Alternatively, the juice may be extracted by pressing the seeds through a fine strainer.

For the granita

5 large (or 7 small) pomegranates

1/2 cup water

1/2 cup sugar

Juice of 1 lemon

For the caramelized grapefruit

3 grapefruits

1 tablespoon brown sugar

1 tablespoon honey

1/2 teaspoon ground allspice

Dash of finely ground black pepper

To make the granita, cut the pomegranates in half crossways, and, working over a bowl, turn the halves inside out, knocking and picking out all the red seeds. Do not include any bits of the bitter white pithy membrane. Transfer the seeds from the bowl to a food mill that is placed over a bowl and turn the handle to extract all the juice from them. Or use a spoon to press and scrape the seeds through a sieve. You should have about 1 1/2 cups of juice. Whisk in the water, sugar, and lemon juice. Pour into a 10-inch square pan with 2-inch-high

sides. Cover and place in the freezer for at least 2 1/2 hours or overnight.

To prepare the caramelized grapefruit, using a sharp chef's knife, trim the tops and bottoms off the grapefruits, exposing the pink flesh. Cut all the peel and white pith off, working your way around the fruits. Section the grapefruits by cutting between each membrane and removing each tender wedge of fruit, working over a bowl so as to catch any dripping juice. Place the sections in the bowl. After removing all the sections, squeeze the remaining inner membrane over the bowl to remove as much juice as possible.

Sprinkle the brown sugar and honey in a sauté pan and place over medium heat. Allow the sugar to melt and begin to brown. When it begins to lightly smoke and is completely melted, carefully add the grapefruit sections and juice, allspice, and pepper, and allow to simmer for 1 1/2 to 2 minutes, stirring carefully, allowing the caramel, spices, and grapefruit juice to reduce and form a light sauce.

Divide the caramelized grapefruit among 8 to 10 bowls. Using the edge of a spoon, scrape shavings off the frozen granita to create a fluffy ice. Make a large scoop of granita and place on top of the caramelized grapefruit. If desired, you may pack the granita into timbale-shaped molds and unmold the timbales on top of the fruit. Serve immediately.

Key Lime Granita with Seasoned Papaya and Banana

Wake up! It's time for dessert! This tangy lime granita sends a jolt through your mouth, balancing out the sweet papaya and banana topping. This dessert plays upon a classic flavor combination. In many tropical countries where papayas are grown, slices of fresh papaya sprinkled with lime juice are often served for dessert or breakfast at local restaurants.

For the granita

8 key limes

2 1/2 cups water

3/4 cup sugar

For the seasoned fruit

1 papaya

4 bananas

1/4 cup honey

2 tablespoons rice vinegar

1/4 teaspoon finely ground black pepper

Dash of salt

To make the granita, using a citrus zester, remove the zest from 2 of the limes and chop finely. Juice all the limes into a medium-sized bowl. Whisk in the water, sugar, and chopped zest. Pour into a 10-inch square pan with 2-inch-high sides, cover, and place in the freezer for at least 2 1/2 hours or overnight.

To prepare the seasoned fruit, peel the papaya, cut in half, and scoop out the black seeds. Cut the fruit into 1- to 2-inch pieces. Peel the bananas and slice in half lengthwise. Cut into angular 1- to 2-inch pieces. Place the fruit in a bowl and toss with the honey, vinegar, pepper, and salt.

Spoon the seasoned fruit into 8 to 10 serving bowls. Using the edge of a spoon, scrape shavings off the frozen granita to create a fluffy ice. Make a large scoop of granita and place on top of the fruit servings. If desired, you may pack the granita into timbale-shaped molds and unmold the timbales on top of the fruit. Serve immediately.

Rafaela who drinks and drinks coconut and papaya juice on Tuesdays and wishes there were sweeter drinks, not bitter like an empty room, but sweet sweet like the island . . .
—SANDRA CISNEROS, "RAFAELA WHO DRINKS COCONUT AND PAPAYA JUICE ON TUESDAYS"

Pineapple Sorbet

MAKES 1 TO 1 1/2 QUARTS, OR **20** TO **25** SERVINGS

The most delicious, fresh pineapples I've ever tasted were the ones Donna and I bought from roadside vendors when we lived in Bénin, West Africa. There was a "pineapple strip" in one of the central pineapple-producing regions of the country, where vendors stacked the fruits into eight-foot-high pyramids lining the road. We bought ten or twelve pineapples at a time, filling a burlap sack with the luscious fruits, loaded them into the back of our bush taxi, and brought them to our village where we ate them for breakfast and dessert for days on end. Unfortunately, we had no electricity or refrigeration, so we never had the means to make a refreshing sorbet like this one!

2 pineapples

1/2 cup orange juice

1/2 cup sugar

Trim the tops and bottoms from the pineapples, then slice all the outer skin from the flesh, working your way around the fruits. Quarter the pineapples lengthwise and trim the core from each quarter. Roughly chop the fruit and place in a blender with the orange juice and sugar. Puree for 30 seconds. Pass through a fine strainer, pressing all juice from the blended flesh through the strainer with a large spoon or ladle. Spin in an ice cream machine according to manufacturer's instructions. Store covered in the freezer.

The Ananas, or pine-apple, is accounted the most delicious fruit, not only of these Islands, but of all America. It is so delightful to the eye and of so sweet a scent that Nature may be said to have been extremely prodigal of what was most rare and precious of her Treasury to this plant.
—CHARLES DE ROCHEFORT,
HISTORY OF THE CARIBBY ISLANDS

Passion Fruit Sorbet

MAKES 1 TO 1 1/2 QUARTS, OR **20** TO **25** SERVINGS

Passion fruits' rich flavors make this one of the most incredible, luscious sorbets you'll ever taste. Its sweet, perfumed citrus flavor refreshingly cleanses your mouth and mind, making it an ideal ending to a spicy meal. I think passion fruits are a delicacy among tropical fruits, and their exquisite taste is best enjoyed to its fullest in this concentrated, flavorful sorbet. It's the ultimate tropical fruit, a must try!

10 passion fruits

3 cups water

1 cup orange juice

1 1/2 cups sugar

Cut the passion fruits in half and scoop the juicy fruit and seed pulp into a blender. Be sure to get every drop of juice into the blender. Add the water, orange juice, and sugar. Pulse the blender on and off at split-second intervals for approximately 15 seconds, just enough to separate the seeds from the pulp. Pass the mixture through a fine strainer to remove the seeds and any large bits of pulp. Spin in an ice cream machine according to manufacturer's instructions. Store covered in the freezer.

Sorbets (clockwise from top): Pineapple, Kumquat-Orange, Grapefruit-Clove, Roasted Banana, and Cactus Pear

Kiwi Sorbet

MAKES 1 TO 11/2 QUARTS, OR 20 TO 25 SERVINGS

Although very familiar to us, the kiwi in our culture has most often been relegated to the role of strawberry sidekick, or used as an often uneaten garnish. In this recipe, the kiwi comes into its own and takes the spotlight. Its sour, tingly flavor and jade-colored flesh make an excellent sorbet, showcasing its greatest assets.

8 to 10 kiwis

1 cup water

11/2 cups sugar

Using a sharp paring knife, peel the kiwis and remove the hard piece of stem at one end. Roughly chop the flesh and place in a blender with the water and sugar. Pulse the blender on and off at split-second intervals for approximately 15 seconds, just enough to separate the seeds from the pulp. Pass the mixture through a fine strainer to remove the seeds and any large bits of pulp. Spin in an ice cream machine according to manufacturer's instructions. Store covered in the freezer.

Cactus Pear Sorbet

MAKES 1 TO 11/2 QUARTS, OR 20 TO 25 SERVINGS

Cactus pears, also called prickly pears, often have interior flesh colored a beautiful magenta pink or garnet red, resembling the color of the desert sun as it rises and sets over the nopales or opuntia cacti that produce this fruit. The flesh might also be green, creating a pale green sorbet resembling the color of honeydew melon. I like to add a little lime juice to this sorbet because its acidity balances out the cactus pear's smooth, sweet flavor.

12 to 14 cactus pears

Juice of 2 limes

1 cup sugar

Use a towel to hold the cactus pears while cutting in order to protect your hands from its small, sharp spines. Cut the pears in half and scoop the inner flesh into a blender. You may either discard the skins or save them to use as serving containers for the finished sorbet. Add the lime juice and sugar to the blender and puree the mixture for 20 seconds. Pass the mixture through a fine strainer. Spin in an ice cream machine according to manufacturer's instructions. Store covered in the freezer.

Guava Sorbet

MAKES 1 TO 11/2 QUARTS, OR 20 TO 25 SERVINGS

Guavas fondly remind me of childhood flavors of bubble gum or sour grape candy, making this sorbet a real treat for kids and adults alike! Buy some guavas and let them ripen in your kitchen—their sweet, floral scent will fill a room with their intense aroma. In Cuba, guavas are the most popular of all fruits, and guava paste or guava jelly, along with Havana cigars, are widely given as presents to friends and relatives who have left the country.

6 guavas

11/2 cups water

1 cup sugar

Juice of 1 lemon

Using a sharp paring knife, peel the guavas and then roughly chop the fruit. Place the fruit in a blender with the water, sugar, and lemon juice. Puree for 30 seconds. Pass the mixture through a fine strainer. Spin in an ice cream machine according to manufacturer's instructions. Store covered in the freezer.

Kumquat-Orange Sorbet

MAKES 1 TO 1 1/2 QUARTS, OR 20 TO 25 SERVINGS

I love the strong, straightforward scent and flavor of kumquats, little oranges that pack a punch. Each miniature fruit delivers a burst of intense orange flavor. This sorbet has a clean and refreshing orange "bite," perfect as an afternoon cooler or palate-cleansing light dessert after a rich meal. The kumquats are first simmered in water to extract bitterness from their skins, and then candied in a simple syrup.

2 cups whole fresh kumquats

7 cups water

2 1/2 cups sugar

3 1/2 cups orange juice

Combine the kumquats and 4 cups of the water in a saucepan and place over medium heat. Simmer the kumquats for 20 to 25 minutes. Drain this water off, retaining the fruit in the pan, and add the remaining 3 cups of water to the pan along with 2 cups of the sugar. Return to medium heat and simmer for 35 to 40 minutes. Drain off the syrup and allow the kumquats to cool.

Prepare the candied kumquats by slicing in half with a paring knife, scraping out and discarding the bitter inner pulp. Combine the kumquat skins, orange juice, and remaining 1/2 cup sugar in a blender. Puree on high speed for 30 to 40 seconds. Pass the mixture through a fine strainer and cool in the refrigerator. Spin in an ice cream machine according to manufacturer's instructions. Store covered in the freezer.

Pepino Melon Sorbet

MAKES 1 TO 1 1/2 QUARTS, OR 20 TO 25 SERVINGS

The sweet yellow flesh of these tropical melons produces a tasty sorbet. Also called melon pears or tree melons, pepino melons are very tiny. Like many small exotic fruits, their intense flavors make up for their size.

3 pepino melons

1/4 cup apple juice

1/2 cup sugar

Trim the skin from the melon flesh, cut in half, and remove seeds with a spoon. Work over a bowl so as to reserve any juice that may drip out while processing the fruit. Roughly chop the fruit and place in a blender with the apple juice, sugar, and any reserved melon juice. Puree for 30 seconds. Pass the mixture through a fine strainer. Spin in an ice cream machine according to manufacturer's instructions. Store covered in the freezer.

Pomegranate Sorbet

The tart scarlet-colored seeds of pomegranates make a striking and refreshing sorbet. Although they can grow as large as an orange, pomegranates are actually members of the berry family. They were widely regarded in the Middle East and Near East as an ancient fertility symbol because of their numerous seeds, and have been considered sacred by many civilizations and cultures. A pomegranate was the symbol for the Greek moon goddess Artemis, and the fruits are also frequently mentioned in the Muslim holy scripture, the Koran. You will need a food mill to crush the juice out of the pomegranate seeds. Alternatively, the juice may be extracted by pressing the seeds through a fine strainer.

8 large (or 10 small) pomegranates

1/2 cup water

1 cup sugar

Juice of 1 lemon

Cut the pomegranates in half crosswise, and, working over a bowl, turn the halves inside out, knocking and picking out all the red seeds. Do not include any bits of the bitter white pithy membrane. Transfer the seeds to a food mill placed over a bowl and turn the handle to extract all their juice, or press and scrape the seeds through a sieve with a large spoon or ladle. (You should have about 2 1/2 cups of juice.) Whisk in the water, sugar, and lemon juice. Pass the mixture through a fine strainer. Spin in an ice cream machine according to manufacturer's instructions. Store covered in the freezer.

Kiwano Melon Sorbet

The golden-orange skins of kiwano melons, also called horned melons, are covered with dull spikes. Native to Africa, they were an important source of food for hunters and gatherers in southern regions of the continent. The green flesh has a flavor resembling banana, watermelon, and cucumber combined. This exotic sorbet makes a wonderful finish to a light summer meal. I like to save the intriguing rind to use as a serving container for the sorbet.

2 kiwano melons

1/2 cup sugar

Juice of 2 limes

Cut the melons in half lengthwise and, using a spoon, scoop all the flesh from the inside of the halves into a blender with the sugar and lime juice. Pulse the blender on and off at split-second intervals for approximately 15 seconds, just enough to separate the seeds from the pulp. Pass the mixture through a fine strainer, squeezing all possible juice from seeds and large bits of pulp. Spin in an ice cream machine according to manufacturer's instructions. Store covered in the freezer.

Tamarillo Sorbet

*MAKES 1 TO 1½ QUARTS, OR **20** TO **25** SERVINGS*

Tamarillos, also called tree tomatoes, are related to tomatoes and egg-plants. Their flesh has a distinctive flavor resembling a cross between tomatoes and cantaloupes. Although the skins can taste bitter when raw, I like to boil them in a simple syrup to extract and sweeten their distinctive flavor before discarding them.

6 tamarillos (tree tomatoes)

1½ cups water

Juice of 1 lemon

1 cup sugar

Cut the tamarillos in half and scoop the flesh into a blender. Place the skins in a saucepan with the water, lemon juice, and sugar and place over medium heat. Bring to a boil, reduce the heat to low, and simmer the mixture for 5 minutes. Remove the skins with a slotted spoon and pour the mixture into the blender with the fruit flesh. Puree for 30 seconds. Pass the mixture through a fine strainer. Spin in an ice cream machine according to manufacturer's instructions. Store covered in the freezer.

Tomatillo Sorbet

*MAKES 1 TO 1½ QUARTS, OR **20** TO **25** SERVINGS*

Although tomatillos are often called Mexican green tomatoes, they're actually related to Cape gooseberries. When I first learned this, I thought they might make a good sorbet and began experimenting. The result was pleasantly surprising, as they produced a delicious sorbet reminiscent of a crisp, tart green apple. I like to serve it scooped into the dried green husks that cover the fruits.

6½ cups whole tomatillos (approximately 2 pounds)

1 cup water

1 cup sugar

½ cup light corn syrup

Clean the tomatillos by soaking in water for a few minutes. Peel the green husks off and set aside to use for serving, if desired. Combine the tomatillos and all remaining ingredients in a blender and puree for 30 to 40 seconds. Pass the mixture through a fine strainer to remove the seeds and any lumps of flesh, and place in the refrigerator to cool. Spin in an ice cream machine according to manufacturer's instructions. Store covered in the freezer.

Grapefruit-Clove Sorbet

Grapefruit sorbet is often served as an intermezzo to cleanse the palate between courses. In this recipe, I spice this familiar sorbet to enhance its astringent fruit flavors with the aromatic, pungent flavor of clove. The result creates a burst of spiced citrus in your mouth, more suitable for dessert than an intermezzo.

4 Ruby Red grapefruits

1/2 cup water

3/4 cup sugar

16 whole cloves

Cut the grapefruits in half and use a small hand-held citrus juicer to squeeze all juice from them. Place the juice in a bowl and set aside. Combine the water, sugar, and cloves in saucepan and place over medium heat. Bring to a boil, reduce heat to low, and simmer for 8 to 10 minutes. Remove the whole cloves with a slotted spoon and whisk the syrup into the grapefruit juice. Spin in an ice cream machine according to manufacturer's instructions. Store covered in the freezer.

> *On Thursday and Friday we purchased many cloves. . . . And for four cubits of Frisian cloth they gave us one bahar of cloves; for two brass chains worth three sols, a hundred pounds of cloves. At length, having no more goods for trade, each man gave them one his cap, another his cloak, and some shirts, amd others clothing, to have his share of cloves.*
> —ANTONIO PIGAFETTA, *MAGELLAN'S VOYAGE*

Roasted Banana Sorbet

*MAKES 1 TO 1 1/2 QUARTS, OR **20** TO **25** SERVINGS*

Bananas that have been roasted in the oven until browned and caramel-colored produce a dark, rich sorbet with a deep banana flavor. This sorbet pairs especially well with chocolate. Serve it with chocolate cake or cookies, or with a scoop of the Chocolate-Cinnamon Ice Cream (page 18).

Vegetable oil

5 ripe bananas

1 1/2 cups water

3/4 cup sugar

Preheat oven to 400°F. Brush a cookie sheet with vegetable oil. Peel the bananas and roughly chop them. Spread the pieces on the oiled cookie sheet and roast in the oven for 40 to 45 minutes, or until bananas are a dark brown caramel color. Remove from the oven and cool for 15 minutes.

Combine the roasted bananas in a blender with the water and sugar. Puree for 30 seconds. Pass the mixture through a fine strainer. Spin in an ice cream machine according to manufacturer's instructions. Store covered in the freezer.

Longan Sorbet

*MAKES 1 TO 1 1/2 QUARTS, OR **20** TO **25** SERVINGS*

Longans, which are nicknamed Dragon's Eyes, make a delicious white sorbet with clean, crisp flavors. The leathery brown skins can be easily removed by squeezing the grape-shaped fruits out of them. Be sure to remove all the inedible black pits inside the fruits. The flavor is similar to lychees, a popular fruit in China.

30 to 35 longans

1/2 cup water

1 cup sugar

Juice of 2 limes

Working over a bowl, squeeze the longan flesh from the brown leathery skins. Cut a slit the length of each fruit and remove the pits. Combine the flesh and juice in a blender with the water, sugar, and lime juice. Puree for 30 seconds. Pass the mixture through a fine strainer. Spin in an ice cream machine according to manufacturer's instructions. Store covered in the freezer.

Coconut Ice Cream

MAKES 1 QUART, OR **16** TO **18** SERVINGS

I think coconuts make the most divine tropical ice cream because their rich, creamy flavor is perfectly suited to it. If you only make one ice cream or sorbet in this book, make this one! It's a fantastic companion to many of the cake, tart, and soup recipes provided here. You can use the reserved coconut water for the Clear Coconut-Guava Soup with Citrus (page 59), or just chill it in the refrigerator for a refreshing drink.

1 large coconut

1 1/2 cups milk

1 cup heavy cream

1/4 cup sugar

4 egg yolks

Preheat oven to 400°F. Poke the "eyes" of the coconut with a blunt tool, like a screwdriver. Drain the coconut water through a strainer into a bowl. Place the whole coconut in the oven and roast for 15 minutes. Remove and allow to cool. Crack it open on a hard surface and pry the flesh from the shell with a spoon. Grate the white flesh using a hand-held grater or a food processor.

Place the grated coconut in a saucepan over medium heat and stir for 5 minutes to help release the coconut milk and natural oils from the flesh. Add the milk and cream and bring to a simmer. Meanwhile, in a bowl, whisk the sugar into the egg yolks until slightly pale and lightened. Pour one-third of the simmered milk mixture into the yolks while stirring with the whisk. Return this mixture to the saucepan, stirring to combine. Stir the custard constantly over medium heat until it thickens to the point where it coats the back of the spoon. Do not allow the custard to boil. Remove from heat and place in the refrigerator to cool for 30 minutes.

When it has cooled, place the coconut custard in a blender and puree at high speed for 40 to 45 seconds. Pass the mixture through a fine strainer. Spin in an ice cream machine according to manufacturer's instructions. Store covered in the freezer.

Chocolate-Cinnamon Ice Cream

MAKES 1 QUART, OR **16** TO **18** SERVINGS

A classic Mexican chocolate preparation contains canela, a type of Mexican cinnamon, and ground almonds. This common, popular flavoring is derived from the Aztec practice of spicing their chocolate drinks with chiles, cinnamon, and occasionally vanilla beans. Enjoy this dessert all by itself or as an accompaniment to a nut dessert, like the Pecan-Molasses Pie (page 83).

1 3/4 cups milk

1 cup heavy cream

6 tablespoons sugar

4 egg yolks

8 ounces bittersweet chocolate, finely chopped

1 tablespoon cocoa powder

2 teaspoons ground cinnamon

Combine the milk and cream in a saucepan and place over medium heat. Bring to a simmer, about 12 to 14 minutes, then remove from the heat. Meanwhile, in a bowl, whisk the sugar into the egg yolks until slightly pale and lightened. Set aside. Whisk the chopped chocolate, cocoa powder, and cinnamon into the simmered milk. Pour one-third of the milk mixture into the yolks while stirring with the whisk. Return this mixture to the saucepan, stirring to combine, and stir the custard constantly over medium heat until it thickens to the point where it coats the back of a spoon, about 6 to 8 minutes. Do not allow the custard to boil. Remove from heat, pass the mixture through a fine strainer, and place in the refrigerator to cool for 30 minutes.

When it has cooled, spin in an ice cream machine according to manufacturer's instructions. Store covered in the freezer.

Sesame Brittle Ice Cream

*MAKES 1 QUART, OR **16** TO **18** SERVINGS*

The toasted flavor of sesame seeds combined with honey or sugar has been enjoyed in Near Eastern and Middle Eastern sweet pastries for centuries. In this recipe, the roasted sesame seeds cut the sweetness of ice cream to create a perfect, nutty harmony. Sesame pairs well with a variety of tropical fruits, including mango, papaya, and citrus fruits.

2 tablespoons sesame seeds

1/4 cup sugar

2 cups milk

1 1/2 cups heavy cream

2 tablespoons honey

5 egg yolks

Brush a cookie sheet with oil and set aside. To make the brittle, toast the sesame seeds in a sauté pan over medium heat, stirring occasionally, for 6 to 8 minutes or until they are light brown. Pour in the sugar, stir, and allow it to melt. When it is browned and lightly smoking, pour the caramelized sugar and sesame seeds onto the prepared cookie sheet. Set the brittle aside to cool.

Combine the milk and cream in a saucepan and place over medium heat. Bring to a simmer, about 12 to 14 minutes, then remove from the heat. While the milk mixture is heating, whisk the honey into the yolks in a bowl until lightened. Pour one-third of the simmered milk mixture into the yolks while stirring with the whisk. Return this mixture to the saucepan, stirring to combine, and stir the custard constantly over medium heat until it thickens to the point where it coats the back of a spoon. Do not allow the custard to boil. Remove from heat, pass the mixture through a fine strainer, and place in the refrigerator to cool for 30 minutes.

When it has cooled, spin in an ice cream machine according to manufacturer's instructions. Pulverize the brittle in a food processor until finely ground. Using a spatula, fold the brittle into the still-soft ice cream. Store covered in the freezer.

Tequila Ice Cream

*MAKES 1 QUART, OR **16** TO **18** SERVINGS*

Tequila is a strong spirit made from the desert blue agave cactus, also known as the maguey. It was named after the town in the Jalisco state of northern Mexico where it originated. Although most people asso-ciate tequila with tart margaritas or shiver-producing shots paired with lime and salt, when sweetened it takes on a floral, musty qual-ity that pairs well with many different tropical fruits.

1 cup milk

1 1/2 cups heavy cream

1/2 cup fine-quality tequila, such as El Tesoro or Herradura

1/4 cup sugar

2 tablespoons honey

4 egg yolks

Combine the milk, cream, and tequila in a saucepan and place over medium heat. Bring to a simmer, about 12 to 14 minutes, then remove from the heat. Meanwhile, in a bowl, whisk the sugar and honey into the egg yolks until slightly pale and lightened. Pour one-third of the milk mixture into the yolks while stirring with the whisk. Return this mixture to the saucepan, stirring to combine, and stir the custard constantly over medium heat until it thickens to the point where it coats the back of a spoon. Do not allow the custard to boil. Remove from heat, pass the mixture through a fine strainer, and place in the refrigerator to cool for 30 minutes.

When it has cooled, spin in an ice cream machine according to manufacturer's instructions. Store covered in the freezer.

Chinese Five-Spice Ice Cream

*MAKES 1 QUART, OR **16** TO **18** SERVINGS*

Chinese five-spice powder is a combination of ground aniseed, fennel seed, clove, cinnamon, and Szechuan pepper that is frequently used in Asian cooking. You can find it in the spice or bulk sections of most natural food stores or Asian specialty stores. When sweetened, the spices make a unique and surprisingly delicious ice cream that matches especially well with fruit tarts, cakes, and compotes.

11/2 cups milk

2 cups heavy cream

1 tablespoon Chinese five-spice powder (or 1/2 teaspoon each of ground aniseed, ground fennel seed, ground clove, ground cinnamon, and finely ground Szechuan pepper)

1/2 cup sugar

6 egg yolks

Combine the milk, cream, and five-spice powder in a saucepan and place over medium heat. Bring to a simmer, about 12 to 14 minutes, then remove from the heat. While the milk mixture is heating, whisk the sugar into the yolks in a bowl until lightened. Pour one-third of the simmered milk mixture into the yolks while stirring with the whisk. Return this mixture to the saucepan, stirring to combine, and stir the custard constantly over medium heat until it thickens to the point where it coats the back of a spoon. Do not allow the custard to boil. Remove from heat, pass the mixture through a fine strainer, and place in the refrigerator to cool for 30 minutes.

When it has cooled, spin in an ice cream machine according to manufacturer's instructions. Store covered in the freezer.

Molasses Ice Cream

*MAKES 1 TO 11/2 QUARTS, OR **20** TO **25** SERVINGS*

Molasses, also called "mother water," is the syrup that is separated from the crystals of raw sugar in the cane refinement process. Use a high-grade molasses with an amber tint for this recipe, and not "blackstrap" molasses, which is the poorest, darkest grade. Some of the best molasses is produced in Louisiana, Puerto Rico, and the Caribbean. I first made this ice cream when I had to make use of four gallons of molasses at Charlie Trotter's restaurant in Chicago. It turned out to be a favorite with the guests, who frequently requested it after it was removed from the menu.

2 cups milk

11/2 cups heavy cream

1/2 cup dark molasses

5 egg yolks

Combine the milk and cream in a saucepan and place over medium heat. Bring to a simmer, about 12 to 14 minutes, then remove from the heat. While the milk mixture is heating, whisk the molasses into the yolks in a bowl until smooth. Pour one-third of the simmered milk mixture into the yolks while stirring with the whisk. Return this mixture to the saucepan, stirring to combine, and stir the custard constantly over medium heat until it thickens to the point where it coats the back of a spoon. Do not allow the custard to boil. Remove from heat, pass the mixture through a fine strainer, and place in the refrigerator to cool for 30 minutes.

When it has cooled, spin in an ice cream machine according to manufacturer's instructions. Store covered in the freezer.

Tropical Nut Brittle Ice Cream

*MAKES 1 QUART, OR **16** TO **18** SERVINGS*

Serve this ice cream on top of Pineapple Spice Cakes (page 73). The mixed roasted premium nuts and sweet brittle crunch make this rich ice cream a harmonious companion to a variety of desserts.

1/2 cup cashews

1/2 cup Brazil nuts

1/2 cup macadamia nuts

1/2 cup sugar

1 1/2 cups milk

1 cup heavy cream

2 tablespoons brown sugar

5 egg yolks

Preheat oven to 350°F. Place the nuts on a cookie sheet and roast for 12 to 14 minutes, until golden brown.

Oil another cookie sheet and set aside. To make the brittle, pour the white sugar into a sauté pan and place over medium heat. Melt the sugar, allowing it to brown and caramelize, about 10 to 12 minutes. When it lightly smokes, stir in the roasted nuts. Pour the caramel-nut brittle mixture onto the oiled cookie sheet and set aside, allowing to cool.

Combine the milk and cream in a saucepan and place over medium heat. Bring to a simmer, about 12 to 14 minutes, then remove from the heat. While the milk mixture is heating, whisk the brown sugar into the yolks in a bowl until lightened. Pour one-third of the simmered milk mixture into the yolks while stirring with the whisk. Return this mixture to the saucepan, stirring to combine, and stir the custard constantly over medium heat until it thickens to the point where it coats the back of a spoon. Do not allow the custard to boil. Remove from heat, pass the mixture through a fine strainer, and place in the refrigerator to cool for 30 minutes.

When it has cooled, spin in an ice cream machine according to manufacturer's instructions. Pulverize the nut brittle in a food processor until finely ground. Using a spatula, fold the brittle into the still-soft ice cream. Store covered in the freezer.

Double Vanilla Ice Cream

*MAKES 1 QUART, OR **16** TO **18** SERVINGS*

Nothing is more versatile than a simple, delicious vanilla ice cream. This recipe packs in plenty of real vanilla flavor! I always say two vanilla beans are better than one, so make it a double!

1 1/2 cups milk

2 cups heavy cream

2 vanilla beans, split and scraped

1/2 cup sugar

6 egg yolks

Combine the milk, cream, and vanilla beans in a saucepan and place over medium heat. Bring to a simmer, about 12 to 14 minutes, then remove from the heat. While the milk mixture is heating, whisk the sugar into the yolks in a bowl until lightened. Pour one-third of the simmered milk mixture into the yolks while stirring with the whisk. Return this mixture to the saucepan, stirring to combine, and stir the custard constantly over medium heat until it thickens to the point where it coats the back of a spoon. Do not allow the custard to boil. Remove from heat and pass the mixture through a fine strainer. Return the vanilla beans to the strained mixture and place in the refrigerator to cool for 30 minutes, allowing the beans to continue steeping and flavoring the custard.

When it has cooled, remove the beans and spin in an ice cream machine according to manufacturer's instructions. Store covered in the freezer.

Cardamom Brittle Ice Cream

*MAKES 1 QUART, OR **16** TO **18** SERVINGS*

Aromatic cardamom is a widely used spice in Indian, Middle Eastern, and North African cuisines. The caramelized crunch of brittle combined with delicate, floral cardamom make this ice cream one of my favorites. Serve it as an accompaniment to citrus, date, and nut desserts. A scoop of this ice cream on top of the Tangerine Tart (page 48) is unforgettable!

1/4 cup sugar

1 tablespoon ground cardamom

1 1/4 cups milk

1 1/4 cups heavy cream

1/4 cup sugar

5 egg yolks

Oil a cookie sheet and set aside. To make the brittle, pour the sugar into a sauté pan and place over medium heat. Melt the sugar, allowing it to brown and caramelize, about 10 to 12 minutes. When it lightly smokes, stir in the cardamom. Pour the caramel brittle mixture onto the oiled cookie sheet and set aside, allowing to cool.

Combine the milk and cream in a saucepan and place over medium heat. Bring to a simmer, about 12 to 14 minutes, then remove from the heat. While the milk mixture is heating, whisk the sugar into the yolks in a bowl until lightened. Pour one-third of the simmered milk mixture into the yolks while stirring with the whisk. Return this mixture to the saucepan, stirring to combine, and stir the custard constantly over medium heat until it thickens to the point where it coats the back of a spoon. Do not allow the custard to boil. Remove from heat, pass the mixture through a fine strainer, and place in the refrigerator to cool for 30 minutes.

When mixture has cooled, spin in an ice cream machine according to manufacturer's instructions. Pulverize the cardamom brittle in a food processor until finely ground. Using a spatula, fold the brittle into the still-soft ice cream. Store covered in the freezer.

Roasted Peanut Ice Cream

*MAKES 1 QUART, OR **16** TO **18** SERVINGS*

In West Africa, market women sell peanuts that they have freshly roasted in the ashes of open fires. I used to buy handfuls of these flavorful West African "groundnuts" for pennies, and munch them while wandering around markets or enjoying Tusk Nigerian beer. This ice cream, inspired by memories of those fresh roasted nuts, is delicious with pineapple, coconut, or chocolate desserts.

2 cups raw peanuts, roasted in a 350°F oven for 10 minutes

2 cups milk

3/4 cup heavy cream

1/2 cup sugar

1/2 teaspoon salt

5 egg yolks

Preheat oven to 350°F. Place the peanuts on a cookie sheet and roast in the oven for 14 to 16 minutes, until dark brown.

Combine the milk and cream in a saucepan and place over medium heat. Bring to a simmer, about 12 to 14 minutes, then remove from the heat. While the milk mixture is heating, whisk the sugar and salt into the yolks in a bowl until lightened. Pour one-third of the simmered milk mixture into the yolks while stirring with the whisk. Return this mixture to the saucepan, stirring to combine, and stir the custard constantly over medium heat until it thickens to the point where it coats the back of a spoon. Do not allow the custard to boil. Remove from heat, pass the mixture through a fine strainer, and place in the refrigerator to cool for 30 minutes.

In a food processor, pulverize the peanuts until ground into a paste and the natural oils have been released, so that the mixture clumps up and resembles crunchy peanut butter. Continue processing while slowly pouring half of the cooled custard into the processor. Process for 30 additional seconds, then add this peanut mixture to the custard and whisk until well combined.

Spin in an ice cream machine according to manufacturer's instructions. Store covered in the freezer.

Piñon-Caramel Ice Cream

*MAKES 1 QUART, OR **16** TO **18** SERVINGS*

Roasted piñons (pine nuts) are a perfect partner for the burned flavor of caramel, recalling the warm, brown shades of arid lands in which piñon trees grow. This ice cream is excellent all by itself, topped with an extra sprinkling of nuts, or with banana, fig, and chocolate desserts. Try it with the Fig and Red Wine Strudel (page 87).

3/4 cup piñons

6 tablespoons sugar

2 1/2 cups heavy cream

1 cup milk

5 egg yolks

Preheat oven to 350°F. Place the piñons on a cookie sheet and roast in the oven for 12 to 14 minutes, until golden brown.

Sprinkle 4 tablespoons of the sugar into a saucepan and place over medium heat. Allow the sugar to melt and caramelize. When it is dark brown and lightly smoking, slowly stir in 1/2 cup of cream. Continue to stir while it splatters and bubbles. When it settles, add the remaining cream and stir. Add the milk and bring the mixture to a simmer, about 12 to 14 minutes, then remove from the heat. While the milk mixture is heating, whisk the remaining 2 tablespoons of sugar into the yolks in a bowl until lightened. Pour one-third of the simmered milk mixture into the yolks while stirring with the whisk. Return this mixture to the saucepan, stirring to combine, and stir the custard constantly over medium heat until it thickens to the point where it coats the back of a spoon. Do not allow the custard to boil. Remove from heat, pass the mixture through a fine strainer, and place in the refrigerator to cool for 30 minutes.

When it has cooled, spin in an ice cream machine according to manufacturer's instructions. Using a spatula, fold the roasted piñons into the still-soft ice cream. Store covered in the freezer.

Ginger-Vanilla Ice Cream Float

*MAKES **6** SERVINGS*

The first dessert I can remember was a special treat my parents fixed for me and my siblings after we returned home from the movie theater in the 1960s: A&W root beer and vanilla ice cream floats served in special, tall glasses with extra-long spoons. These float recipes are my interpretations of this warm childhood memory of a cold delight! This one uses homemade ginger soda instead of A&W root beer—a refreshing tropical substitution.

1/2 cup grated gingerroot

1/4 cup honey

2 teaspoons lemon juice

1/2 cup water

Grind of black pepper

24 ounces sparkling water, such as San Pellegrino or Perrier

**1 recipe Double Vanilla Ice Cream (page 21)
   or 1 pint store-bought vanilla ice cream**

Combine the grated ginger, honey, lemon juice, water, and black pepper in a saucepan and place over medium heat. Simmer for 4 to 6 minutes. When cool, pass through a strainer into a pitcher and fill with the sparkling water.

Place 2 scoops of ice cream into 6 individual tall glasses. Pour the ginger soda into the glasses. Serve with straws and long spoons.

> *I must have saffron to colour the warden pies;*
> *mace—dates—none; that's out of my note;*
> *nutmegs, seven; a race or two of ginger—but that*
> *I may beg; four pounds of prunes, and as many*
> *raisins o' th' sun.*
> —WILLIAM SHAKESPEARE, *THE WINTER'S TALE 4.2*

Pineapple-Coconut
Ice Cream Float

*MAKES **6** SERVINGS*

This delicious float is reminiscent of the popular piña colada drink, with fresh pineapple and dreamy coconut ice cream. It's an excellent dessert for a summertime lunch, or a lazy afternoon lounging in the sun.

1 large pineapple

1 cup brown sugar

1 teaspoon vanilla extract

1 cup orange juice

24 ounces sparkling water, such as San Pellegrino or Perrier

1 recipe Coconut Ice Cream (page 18) or 1 pint store-bought ice cream

1 cup Coconut Shavings (optional), roasted at 350°F for 12 to 14 minutes

Using a sharp chef's knife, trim the top and bottom off the pineapple and then slice off the skin, working around the fruit until finished. Quarter the pineapple by cutting lengthwise from top to bottom. Trim the core from each quarter and roughly chop the fruit. Place the pineapple in a blender with the brown sugar, vanilla, and orange juice. Puree on high speed for 15 seconds. Pass the mixture through a fine strainer into a pitcher and fill with sparkling water.

Place 2 scoops of coconut ice cream into 6 individual tall glasses. Fill with pineapple soda and top with coconut shavings, if desired. Serve with straws and long spoons.

Fruit Punch–Tequila
Ice Cream Float

*MAKES **6** SERVINGS*

If you're tempted to try making Tequila Ice Cream (page 19) but aren't sure how to serve it, brighten up a summer afternoon with these fruity floats! I think tequila and tropical fruits make a compelling combination, with a nice balance of floral and fruit flavors. For a fruit punch that packs an extra punch, add a splash of tequila!

2 guavas or 2 feijoas, peeled

1 mango, peeled and cut from pit

2 cactus pears, peeled, or 1 papaya, peeled and seeded

1 banana, peeled

1/4 cup sugar

1 cup orange juice

24 ounces sparkling water, such as San Pellegrino or Perrier

1 recipe Tequila Ice Cream (page 19) or 1 pint store-bought rum raisin ice cream

Roughly chop all the peeled fruit and place in a blender with the sugar and orange juice. Puree for 20 to 30 seconds. Pass through a fine strainer into a pitcher. Fill with sparkling water.

Place 2 scoops of the ice cream into 6 individual tall glasses. Fill with the fruit punch and serve with straws and long spoons.

Ice Cream Floats: Pineapple-Coconut (l.)
and Fruit Punch–Tequila (r.)

Ginger-Honey Pound Cake Sundae

Pound cakes earned their name because they were originally made with one pound flour, one pound butter, one pound sugar, and one pound eggs. In this recipe, a much lighter version of this traditional household cake is flavored with ginger, vanilla, and honey, then topped with vanilla ice cream and a caramelized honey sauce, a delicious testament to the classic cake and ice cream combination!

For the pound cake

1 cup all-purpose flour

1/4 teaspoon salt

1/4 teaspoon baking soda

1 teaspoon ground ginger

1/4 cup sour cream

1/2 cup heavy cream

1/2 cup (1 stick) unsalted butter, softened

1/2 cup sugar

1/4 cup honey

3 eggs

2 tablespoons grated gingerroot

1/2 teaspoon vanilla extract

For the dark honey sauce

3/4 cup honey

1/2 cup water

For the whipped cream

1/2 cup heavy cream

1 tablespoon powdered sugar

1/4 teaspoon vanilla extract

**1 recipe Double Vanilla Ice Cream (page 21)
   or 1 pint store-bought vanilla ice cream**

To make the pound cake, preheat oven to 350°F. Sift together the flour, salt, baking soda, and dried ginger in a bowl and set aside. Stir together the sour cream and cream in a separate bowl and set aside. Using a mixer, cream the butter with the sugar until light in color. Add the honey and continue mixing for 3 to 4 minutes. Add the eggs one at a time, then the fresh grated ginger, while continuing to mix on low speed. Add one-half of the dry ingredients and mix until well combined, then add one-half of the sour cream–cream mixture and mix until well combined. Repeat process, adding the remaining dry and wet ingredients and vanilla extract, and continue mixing until smooth.

Prepare an 8×4×4-inch loaf pan by greasing with butter or oil and dusting with flour. Pour the pound cake batter into the pan and bake for 1 hour, or until a knife inserted in the center comes out clean. Allow the cake to cool for 10 minutes, then remove from the pan.

While the cake is baking, prepare the dark honey sauce and whipped cream. Place the honey in a saucepan over medium heat. Allow the honey to bubble and simmer. When it darkens to a caramel color, about 14 to 16 minutes, remove from heat. Using special care because the mixture will splatter, pour the water into the honey and stir with a whisk until smooth. If the honey clumps up, return the pan to the heat and stir until smooth. Remove from heat, and allow the sauce to cool. Set aside until ready to serve.

Using a mixer, whip the cream with the powdered sugar and vanilla extract until it forms stiff peaks. Set aside or refrigerate until ready to serve. When ready to serve, cut the pound cake into 1-inch-thick slices and place on individual plates. Top each slice with a scoop of vanilla ice cream, a dollop of whipped cream, and a drizzle of dark honey sauce.

Ginger-Honey Pound Cake Sundae

Chocolate-Kumquat Bombe

Bombes, coupes, and parfaits were some of the first frozen desserts served when ice creams and sorbets were introduced to Europeans in the 17th century by those who learned of them while traveling in China and Arab countries. Ice bombes, traditional molded frozen desserts filled with two flavors of ice cream, were customarily served as dessert for any kind of special 18th-century dinner in France. In this bombe with a tropical twist, rich chocolate ice cream is paired with the bright citrus flavors of kumquat and orange.

1 recipe Chocolate-Cinnamon Ice Cream (page 18), omitting the cinnamon, or 1 pint store-bought chocolate ice cream, slightly softened

1 recipe Kumquat-Orange Sorbet (page 13)

Brush a bread loaf pan or terrine mold lightly with oil and then line it with a piece of plastic wrap large enough to fold over the top of the pan. Spread a 1/2- to 1-inch layer of chocolate ice cream covering the bottom and sides of the pan. Place in the freezer and allow to chill for 1/2 hour, or until the ice cream is firmly frozen.

Remove from freezer and fill the middle with Kumquat-Orange sorbet. Fold the extra plastic wrap over the top of the bombe and press firmly to squeeze out any small air bubbles. Return to freezer and chill until well set, about 1 1/2 to 2 hours.

When ready to serve, remove the bombe from freezer and peel the plastic wrap off the top. Invert the pan onto a chilled plate or cutting surface, and carefully remove the entire piece of plastic wrap. Dip a sharp chef's knife into hot water to warm it, and cut a slice from the bombe. Rinse the knife in hot water and repeat until desired number of slices have been cut. Serve the bombe slices immediately on well-chilled plates.

Chocolate-Kumquat Bombe

Mango, Blood Orange, and Pistachio Cassata

MAKES 8 SERVINGS

Cassatas are rectangular-shaped frozen desserts originating in Italy, made with layers of fruit-flavored whipped cream or ice cream. The name means "little case," referring to the bricklike shape of the desserts. This cassata combines the classic Middle Eastern combination of pistachio and orange with the sweet, floral flavor of mango. It makes a beautiful dessert, with contrasting layers of orange, red, and pale green.

1 1/4 cups pistachios, shelled

1 mango

4 blood oranges

3 cups heavy cream

1/4 cup sugar

Preheat oven to 350°F. Spread the pistachios on a cookie sheet and roast in the oven for 14 to 16 minutes. Remove from oven and set aside to cool.

Peel the mango and cut the flesh from the pit. Puree in a food processor, and transfer to a bowl. Using a sharp chef's knife, trim the tops and bottoms off the blood oranges, then cut all the peel and pith from the inner flesh, working your way around the fruit. Section the oranges by cutting between each membrane and removing each wedge of fruit. Puree the orange sections in a food processor, and transfer to a second bowl. Clean and dry the food processor, and pulverize the pistachios until very fine. Transfer the ground nuts to a third bowl.

In another bowl, whip the cream and sugar until it forms stiff peaks. Divide the whipped cream between the three bowls containing mango, orange, and pistachio, and using a rubber spatula, gently fold each mixture until combined.

Brush an 8×4×4-inch loaf pan with oil and line with plastic wrap, pressing firmly into the corners to remove any air bubbles. Use a large piece of plastic wrap so that is folds over the top of the pan. Pour the mango mixture into the bottom and spread evenly with the spatula. Place in the freezer for 1/2 hour. (Note: Store the remaining whipped cream mixtures in the refrigerator while freezing each layer.) Remove from freezer, pour in the pistachio mixture, and spread evenly. Return to the freezer for another 1/2 hour. When the pistachio layer is well set, pour the blood orange mixture on top and spread evenly. Fold the extra plastic wrap over the top of the cassata and press firmly to squeeze out any small air bubbles. Return to the freezer for 1 1/2 to 2 hours.

When ready to serve, remove the cassata from the freezer and peel the plastic wrap off the top. Invert the pan onto a chilled plate or cutting surface, and carefully remove the entire piece of plastic wrap. Dip a sharp chef's knife into hot water to warm it, and slice the cassata crosswise. Rinse the knife in hot water and repeat until desired number of slices have been cut. Serve the slices immediately on well-chilled plates.

Mango, Blood Orange, and Pistachio Cassata

Frozen Hawaii

This dessert is my version of the polar opposite of Baked Alaska—what could be more refreshing than a crisp, cool granita, rich ice cream, and tropically spiced cake in hot Hawaii? This delicious cake is flavored with allspice, cinnamon, and vanilla and then covered with a layer of frozen pineapple granita. Serve it topped with decadent Coconut Ice Cream (page 18) and sprinkled with roasted macadamia nuts. You can make the cake and granita well ahead of time, and assemble the final dessert in the last hour before serving.

For the spice cake

3 eggs

1/2 cup brown sugar

1/2 cup flour

1 teaspoon ground cinnamon

1 teaspoon ground allspice

1 teaspoon vanilla extract

1 tablespoon unsalted butter, melted

For the pineapple granita

1 pineapple

1/4 cup orange juice

2 tablespoons brown sugar

To serve

1 recipe Coconut Ice Cream (page 18) or Double Vanilla Ice Cream (page 21) or 1 pint store-bought vanilla ice cream

1/2 cup macadamia nuts, roasted and crushed (optional)

To make the spice cake, preheat oven to 375°F. Using a mixer, whip the eggs and brown sugar at high speed for 5 to 6 minutes until eggs are very light and have soft peaks. In a separate bowl, stir together the flour, cinnamon, and allspice. Sift one-third of the dry ingredients over the whipped eggs and use a spatula to carefully fold together. Repeat with the remaining two-thirds of the dry mixture. Take caution to fold the batter with a light touch, so as not to knock out the air trapped inside the whipped eggs. Stir together the vanilla extract and melted butter in a separate bowl. Add one-third of the cake batter to it and gently fold together. Return this mixture to the remaining batter and fold with 3 or 4 gentle strokes.

Prepare a 10-inch round cake pan by greasing with butter or oil and dusting with flour, tapping out any excess. Pour the batter into the pan, smooth and evenly distribute with a spatula, and bake for 20 to 22 minutes. Allow the cake to cool in the pan on rack.

To make the granita, using a sharp chef's knife, trim the top and bottom off the pineapple and then slice off the skin, working around the fruit until finished. Quarter the pineapple by cutting lengthwise from top to bottom. Trim the core from each quarter and roughly chop the fruit. Place the chopped pineapple in a blender with the orange juice and brown sugar, and puree for 30 seconds. Pour the puree into a large pan with approximately 2-inch-high sides, cover with plastic wrap, and place in the freezer. Allow the granita to freeze for 2 1/2 to 3 hours.

About 1 hour before serving, remove the granita from the freezer and allow it to soften slightly at room temperature for a few minutes. Use a spoon to scrape the softened granita into a fluffy mixture. Remove the spice cake from its pan and place it on a serving plate. Use a metal spatula to spread a 1/2-inch layer of granita over the top of the cake. Return the cake to the freezer for 1/2 hour, until the granita is well set on top of it. Remove it from the freezer, dip a sharp chef's knife into hot water to warm it, and cut the cake into 8 pieces. Use a spatula to place the pieces on plates, and top with a scoop of coconut or vanilla ice cream. Sprinkle with roasted, crushed macadamia nuts, if desired. Serve immediately.

Kiwano Boat Sundae

This colorful, fun sundae is certain to stimulate conversation! A simple combination of Kiwano Melon Sorbet (page 14) with one or two other sorbets or ice creams is served with fresh mango and pineapple in exotic-looking bright orange, spiked kiwano melon rinds—a delightful end to a summertime lunch or dinner party. These boats will surely float!

1 recipe Kiwano Melon Sorbet, with melon rinds reserved (page 14)

1 additional flavor tropical sorbet of your choice

1 flavor ice cream of your choice

1 kiwano melon

1 pineapple

1 mango

When preparing the Kiwano Melon Sorbet, be sure to reserve the four melon halves.

Cut the single kiwano melon in half lengthwise, use a spoon to scrape out the seeds and pulp, and place the two halves with the four reserved melon halves from the sorbet recipe. Cut a small slice off the bottom of each melon half, so that when laid flat they do not roll around.

Using a sharp chef's knife, trim the top and bottom off the pineapple and then slice off the skin, working around the fruit until finished. Quarter the pineapple by cutting lengthwise from top to bottom. Trim the core from each quarter and roughly chop the fruit into 1/2-inch pieces. Peel the mango, cut the flesh from the center pit, and roughly chop into 1/2-inch pieces.

Divide the chopped fruit between the 6 kiwano "boats" and place on plates. Top with an assortment of sorbets and/or ice creams, and serve.

Red Banana Split

*MAKES **6** SERVINGS*

Red bananas are one of the most flavorful varieties of this popular and widespread tropical fruit. Their vibrant flavor makes an exceptional banana split! For a rich, decadent dessert, use the Chocolate-Cinnamon Ice Cream (page 18) and Roasted Banana Sorbet (page 17). For something on the lighter side, try Double Vanilla Ice Cream (page 21) with any of the simple fruit sorbets.

For the split

6 red bananas

1/4 cup sugar

2 tablespoons brandy or dark rum

1 to 3 flavors of ice cream or sorbet of your choice

1/2 cup cashews, roasted and lightly crushed (optional)

For the chocolate sauce

1/2 cup hot water

6 ounces bittersweet chocolate (or 1 1/2 cups chopped), melted

For the whipped cream

1/2 cup heavy cream

2 tablespoons sugar

1/2 teaspoon vanilla extract

Peel the bananas and cut them in half lengthwise. Pour the 1/4 cup sugar in a large sauté pan and place over medium heat. When the sugar is melted, caramelized, and beginning to lightly smoke, carefully add the brandy. Take caution, as the mixture will initially bubble and splatter. Add the banana halves and gently cook them, stirring in the caramel, turning with a spoon from side to side, until they are softened and have taken on some of the caramel color and flavor, approximately 6 to 7 minutes. Remove the pan from the heat.

For the sauce, whisk the hot water into the melted chocolate until smooth. Set aside. For the whipped cream, whip the cream with the sugar and vanilla extract until stiff peaks are formed.

Divide the caramelized bananas between 6 bowls, laying them parallel with their cut sides facing up. Place 1 to 3 scoops of ice cream on the bananas, drizzle with chocolate sauce, and top with a dollop of whipped cream. Sprinkle with some crushed, roasted cashews, if desired.

Red Banana Split

Red Moon Pistachio-Plum Cake

MAKES A *10*-INCH ROUND CAKE, OR **10** SERVINGS

Although plums aren't tropical, they pair very well with pistachio nuts, allspice, ginger, citrus, and vanilla—all tropical products. Plums are used extensively in Asian cooking, and add a fruity twist to this delicious, spiced cake. Use the separated egg yolks for a batch of Double Vanilla Ice Cream (page 21) to serve with the cake.

For the cake

1 1/2 cups pistachios, shelled

1 cup sugar

1 1/4 cups all-purpose flour

2 teaspoons ground allspice

6 egg whites

1 cup unsalted butter, melted

1 tablespoon honey

6 plums

1 quart water for blanching

1 quart ice water for plunging

For the poaching liquid

2 cups sake or white wine, such as Sauvignon Blanc

1 cup orange juice

2 teaspoons vanilla extract

1/2 cup sugar

1 tablespoon grated gingerroot

1/2 teaspoon finely ground black pepper

For the cake, preheat oven to 350°F. Spread the pistachios on a cookie sheet and lightly roast in the oven for 14 to 16 minutes. Allow to cool briefly, then place in a food processor and pulverize until finely ground. Combine the pistachios in a large bowl with the sugar, flour, and allspice. Stir together, breaking up any clumps of nuts with your fingers.

Using a mixer, whip the egg whites at high speed until very frothy but not yet forming soft peaks. Set aside. In a separate bowl, stir together the butter and honey. Stir the butter mixture into the dry ingredients, then fold in the whipped egg whites until the mixture is thoroughly combined. Set aside.

To prepare the poached plums, place one quart of water in a saucepan over high heat and bring to a boil. Using a paring knife, cut an X through the skin of each plum and plunge the fruits into the boiling water. Leave them for 45 seconds, then use a slotted spoon to remove them from the boiling water and plunge them into a bowl of ice water. Allow to sit for one minute. The plum skins should easily peel off the fruits. If they are difficult to remove in spots, peel the skin off with a paring knife. Remove the plum stones, or pits, by holding the fruits in your hand and inserting a melon baller into the stem ends to scoop them out. You should be able to loosen the stones by turning the melon baller around them, then pulling them free.

Combine the sake or white wine, orange juice, vanilla extract, sugar, ginger, and black pepper in a saucepan and place over medium heat. Bring to a simmer, reduce the heat to low, and add the whole, skinned and pitted plums to poach them. If the fruits are very ripe and tender, turn the heat off as soon as you add the plums to the poaching liquid. If they are firm, poach the plums at a low simmer until softened, about 12 to 15 minutes depending on ripeness. Remove from heat.

Preheat oven to 375°F. Prepare an 8- to 10-inch springform pan or a 10-inch round cake pan by greasing with butter or oil and dusting with flour, tapping out any excess. Place the whole poached plums in a circle in the pan, reserving the poaching liquid to use as a sauce. Pour the cake batter over and around the plums. Bake on the middle rack of the oven for 40 to 45 minutes, or until a knife inserted into the cake comes out clean. Cool in the pan on a rack, then invert onto a cake plate or serving dish. Cut the cake into wedges, divide them between individual plates, and spoon some of the reserved poaching liquid over and around each piece.

Macadamia–Coconut Cream Cake
with Mango, Papaya, and Carambola

*MAKES A 10-INCH ROUND CAKE, OR **10** SERVINGS*

This cake was inspired by a dessert from Chez Panisse, Alice Waters's famous Berkeley restaurant. We also served a version of it at Charlie Trotter's in Chicago, which we "frosted" with whipped cream at the last minute and served on dramatic black plates, splattered with melted white chocolate and colorful tropical fruits. This recipe is much simpler, and makes a light, easy dessert that is perfect for large celebratory gatherings.

For the cake

2 cups macadamia nuts

1 cup all-purpose flour

6 eggs, separated

1 1/2 cups sugar

2 teaspoons dark rum (optional)

2 tablespoons unsalted butter, melted

For the whipped cream icing and fruit topping

2 cups heavy cream

1/4 cup sugar

2 teaspoons vanilla extract

1 mango

1 papaya

1 carambola (starfruit)

2 cups coconut shavings, roasted at 350°F for 12 to 14 minutes

To make the cake, preheat oven to 350°F. Spread the macadamia nuts on a cookie sheet and lightly roast in the oven for 14 to 16 minutes, or until golden brown. Remove the nuts from the oven and increase the temperature to 375°F. Allow the nuts to briefly cool, then combine them in a food processor with the flour. Pulse the processor several times to break the nuts into pieces without pulverizing them too much. Set aside.

Using a mixer, whip the egg yolks at high speed with 3/4 cup of the sugar until light and thick, about 6 to 8 minutes. Add

the rum, if desired, and melted butter and mix for only a few seconds, just enough to combine. In a separate bowl, whip the egg whites, sprinkling in the remaining 3/4 cup sugar after the first minute, and continuing to whip at high speed until stiff peaks form. Fold the nut mixture into the yolks until combined, then gently fold this into the whipped egg whites until smooth.

Prepare a 10-inch round cake pan by greasing with butter or oil and dusting with flour, tapping out any excess. Pour the batter into the pan and spread evenly with a spatula. Bake for 25 to 30 minutes, or until a knife inserted in the center of the cake comes out clean. Allow the cake to cool thoroughly in its pan.

While the cake is baking, prepare the whipped cream and fruits. Whip the cream with the sugar and vanilla extract until stiff peaks form. Set aside. Peel the mango, cut the flesh from the center pit, and chop the fruit into 1-inch-sized chunks. Peel the papaya, cut it in half lengthwise, scrape out the black seeds and cut the fruit into 1-inch-sized chunks. Wash the carambola and cut crosswise into 1/4-inch-thick, star-shaped slices. Carefully remove seeds in each slice with a paring knife. Toss the fruit together in a bowl and set aside.

To assemble the cake, using a serrated knife, slice the cooled cake in half crosswise, creating two layers. Place the bottom half on a cake plate or serving dish. Spread a 1/4- to 1/2-inch layer of whipped cream on top of this layer, and gently cover with the second layer of cake. Cover the sides and top of the cake with the remaining whipped cream. Press roasted coconut shavings against the sides, and place the cake in the refrigerator to chill for at least 20 minutes. Cut and serve the cake with the mixed tropical fruits served on top and around the individual slices.

Yellow Half-Moon Brazil Nut Peach Cake

Like plums, peaches are not a tropical fruit but make an excellent companion to Brazil nuts and tropical spices. This cake is a playful adaptation of a classic Chinese pastry called Moon Cake. My yellow half-moons are halved peaches, enshrined in a moist cake flavored with Brazil nuts, coriander, and ginger, and served with a simple gingered sake-peach sauce.

For the cake

1 1/2 cups Brazil nuts

1 cup sugar

1 1/4 cups all-purpose flour

1 teaspoon ground coriander (optional)

1 teaspoon ground ginger

6 egg whites

1 cup unsalted butter, melted

1 tablespoon honey

3 large or 4 to 5 small peaches

1 quart water for blanching

1 quart ice water for plunging

For the sauce

1 peach

1/4 to 1/2 cup sake or white wine

2 tablespoons brown sugar

2 teaspoons finely grated gingerroot

For the cake, preheat oven to 350°F. Spread the Brazil nuts on a cookie sheet and lightly roast in the oven for 14 to 16 minutes, or until golden brown. Allow to briefly cool, then place in a food processor and pulverize until finely ground. Combine the nuts in a large bowl with the sugar, flour, coriander, and ground ginger. Stir together, breaking up any clumps of nuts with your fingers.

Using a mixer, whip the egg whites at high speed until very frothy but not yet forming soft peaks. Set aside. In a separate small bowl, stir together the melted butter and honey. Stir the butter mixture into the dry ingredients, then fold in the whipped egg whites until the entire mixture is thoroughly combined. Set this batter aside.

Place one quart of water in a saucepan over high heat and bring to a boil. Using a paring knife, cut an X through the skin of the 6 peaches and plunge the fruits into the boiling water. Leave them for 45 seconds, then use a slotted spoon to remove them from the boiling water and plunge them into a bowl of ice water. Allow to sit for one minute. The peach skins should easily peel off the fruits. If they are difficult to remove in spots, peel the skin off with a paring knife. Cut the peeled peaches in half, top to bottom, and remove the stones (pits) with a paring knife. Set aside.

Preheat oven to 375°F. Prepare an 8- to 10-inch springform pan or a 10-inch round cake pan by greasing with butter or oil and dusting with flour, tapping out any excess. Place the peeled, half peaches with cut side facing up in a circle in the pan. Pour the cake batter over and around the fruit. Bake on the middle rack of the oven for 40 to 45 minutes, or until a knife inserted into the cake comes out clean. Cool in the pan on a rack.

You can prepare the sauce while the cake is baking. Cut the remaining single, unpeeled peach in half and remove the stone. Roughly chop the fruit and place in a blender with 1/4 cup sake or white wine, brown sugar, and grated ginger. Add more sake or wine as is needed until the sauce has a thin, runny consistency. Set aside.

When ready to serve, invert the cooled cake onto a cake plate or cutting surface. Cut it into wedges, divide the wedges between individual plates, and spoon some spiced peach sauce over and around each piece.

Three-Spice Cake with Figs and Oranges

I love spice cakes because they are always bursting with flavor and are never bland. This Middle Eastern–influenced cake is spiced with cardamom, nutmeg, and ginger, with figs and orange sections folded into the batter. If you can't find figs, which are available intermittently through summer and fall, you can substitute papaya or banana.

1 cup (2 sticks) unsalted butter

2 cups all-purpose flour

2 teaspoons baking soda

1 teaspoon salt

1 teaspoon ground cardamom

1 teaspoon ground nutmeg

1 teaspoon ground ginger

1 cup almonds, roasted at 350°F for 12 to 14 minutes
  and then finely ground

1 1/2 cups sugar

4 eggs

4 figs, preferably Black Mission

2 large oranges

Powdered sugar for dusting

Preheat the oven to 300°F. Place the butter in a saucepan over medium heat. Allow it to cook after melting, until lightly browned and emitting a nutty scent, about 6 to 8 minutes. Turn off the heat and allow the browned butter to cool.

In a bowl, sift together the flour, baking soda, salt, and spices, and stir in the ground almonds. Pour the browned butter into a mixer equipped with a whip attachment. Add the sugar and whip on high speed. Add the eggs one at a time, at 30-second intervals, while continuing to whip. Fold the dry mixture into the butter-egg mixture until thoroughly combined. Set aside.

Cut the hard stems off the figs and cut each fruit lengthwise into 6 wedges. Using a sharp chef's knife, trim the tops and bottoms off the oranges, then cut all the peel and pith from the flesh, working your way around the fruit. Section the oranges by cutting between each membrane and removing each wedge of fruit. Fold the fig wedges and orange sections into the batter.

Prepare a 10-inch round cake or springform pan by greasing with butter or oil and dusting with flour, tapping out any excess. Pour the batter into the pan and bake for 1 hour, or until a knife inserted into the center comes out clean. Cool the cake in the pan on a rack. When cooled, invert it onto a cake pan or serving dish. Sift powdered sugar over the top to lightly dust it. Serve with Double Vanilla Ice Cream (page 21) or store-bought ice cream of your choice.

Guava–Strawberry Cream Roll

Guavas and strawberries are a classic south-of-the-border combination. I first tasted a dessert similar to this one in a Mexican restaurant in a Latino Chicago neighborhood. A light sponge cake is rolled with guava cream and fresh, sliced strawberries. Serve topped with additional fresh strawberries and a scoop of Guava Sorbet (page 12) for a wonderful Sunday brunch dessert.

For the cake

1 egg

2 egg yolks

1/2 cup sugar

3 egg whites

3/4 cup all-purpose flour

For the filling

1 pint strawberries

1 1/2 cups heavy cream

3 guavas

1/2 cup sugar

1 teaspoon vanilla extract

To make the cake, preheat oven to 400°F. Using a mixer, whip the whole egg, 2 yolks, and 1/4 cup of the sugar at high speed for 5 minutes, until the color is lightened and consistency is very thick. In a separate mixing bowl, whip the egg whites at high speed until soft peaks form, then sprinkle in the remaining sugar and continue whipping until stiff peaks form. Fold half of the whipped egg whites into the yolk mixture, then sift approximately half of the flour into the mixture and combine. Add the remaining egg whites, then the remaining flour, and fold just enough to gently incorporate all the ingredients while still maintaining the airy volume of the egg whites.

Prepare a 10×14×1-inch cookie sheet by greasing with butter or oil and dusting with flour, tapping out any excess. Turn the batter into the pan and evenly distribute it with a spatula. Bake for 7 to 8 minutes, or until the cake springs back when lightly touched. Allow to cool in the pan on a rack.

To prepare the filling, wash, hull, and slice the strawberries 1/4 to 1/8 inch thick. Using a mixer, whip the cream to stiff peaks and set aside. Peel the guavas, roughly chop the flesh, and puree it in a food processor with the sugar and vanilla. Pass the puree through a fine strainer to remove the seeds. Fold the strained puree into the whipped cream, then fold in the sliced strawberries.

To assemble the cake, turn the baked cake out onto a piece of waxed paper or plastic wrap, bottom-side up. Using a rubber spatula, spread the guava and strawberry cream over the surface of the cake. Starting from a long edge, gently roll the cake to the opposite edge. Carefully transfer it to a cake plate or serving dish and chill in the refrigerator until ready to serve.

Guava–Strawberry Cream Roll

White Chocolate Tropical Torte

*MAKES A 10-INCH ROUND CAKE, OR **10** SERVINGS*

For the cake

3/4 cup cashews, macadamias, or Brazil nuts

3/4 cup powdered sugar

4 eggs

1/4 cup all-purpose flour

3 egg whites

3 tablespoons sugar

3 tablespoons unsalted butter, melted

For the icing

8 ounces white chocolate

1 teaspoon powdered unflavored gelatin

3/4 cup heavy cream

2 egg whites

3 to 4 cups assorted peeled, seeded and cut-up tropical fruits, such as:
Mango, Papaya, Carambola (starfruit), Cherimoya, Passion fruits, Kiwi, and Pineapple

1 cup roasted coconut shavings

To make the cake, preheat oven to 350°F. Spread the nuts on a dry cookie sheet and roast for 14 to 16 minutes, until golden brown. Remove them from the oven and set aside to briefly cool. Increase the oven temperature to 375°F.

Pulverize the roasted nuts with the powdered sugar in a food processor. Crack the eggs into a mixing bowl and add the nut mixture. Whip at high speed for 5 minutes, until the volume has increased and mixture is light in color. Sift the flour over the egg mixture and fold in with a spatula until just combined. Set aside. In a separate mixing bowl, whip the egg whites until soft peaks form, then sprinkle in the sugar and continue whipping until stiff peaks form. Gently fold the whipped whites into the egg-nut mixture until combined. Add the melted butter and combine with a few gentle folds.

Prepare a 10-inch round cake pan by greasing with butter or oil and dusting with flour, tapping out any excess. Turn the batter into the pan and distribute evenly with a spatula. Bake for 25 to 30 minutes, or until cake springs back when lightly touched. Allow cake to thoroughly cool in pan on a rack.

For the icing, roughly chop the white chocolate into pieces and place in a double boiler over medium heat. (The water in the bottom portion should not boil.) Stir the chocolate occasionally until it is completely melted. Set aside to cool.

In a saucepan, sprinkle the gelatin over 2 tablespoons of cool water to let it "bloom" for 1 minute. Add 1/4 cup of the cream and place the saucepan over low heat. Allow the mixture to get very hot, stirring periodically. When the gelatin has completely dissolved, remove from heat and whisk this mixture into the melted white chocolate until thoroughly combined. Refrigerate until cool to the touch.

In separate bowls, whip the remaining cream until stiff peaks form, then whip the egg whites to stiff peaks. When the white chocolate mixture is at room temperature or cool to the touch, fold both the whipped cream and whipped whites into the chocolate until smooth. Place in the refrigerator to chill for at least 1/2 hour. While this mixture cools, you can prepare your fresh fruits. Work over a large bowl while peeling and cutting the fruits, so you can reserve the juices.

To assemble the cake, turn the cake out of its pan and use a serrated knife to slice it in half crosswise, making two layers. Drizzle the two cake layers with the fruit juices. Place the bottom layer on a cake plate or serving dish, and spread an even layer of white chocolate icing over the layer. Cover with the top cake layer, and ice the sides and top of the entire cake with the remaining white chocolate mixture. Smooth out the surface with a long, metal spatula dipped in hot water. Gently cover the top and sides with a colorful assortment of sliced tropical fruits and roasted coconut shavings. Chill the cake for at least 20 minutes before serving.

White Chocolate Tropical Torte

Avocado Tart

Although we usually enjoy avocados in the manner of vegetables, they are subtropical fruits. I've always been tempted to create a satisfying dessert from avocados, and this recipe is it! The creamy, rich avocado custard of this tart, flavored with lime juice and nutmeg, is outstanding with fresh citrus fruits, kiwis, or passion fruits.

For the crust

1/2 cup (1 stick) unsalted butter

1 1/4 cups all-purpose flour

1 teaspoon ground cumin

1/2 teaspoon salt

1 teaspoon sugar

1/4 cup ice water

For the filling

2 ripe Haas avocados

Juice of 2 limes

3 eggs

1/2 cup sugar

1/2 cup heavy cream

1/2 cup milk

1/4 teaspoon salt

1/2 teaspoon ground nutmeg

1/4 teaspoon allspice

To make the crust, cut the butter into 1/2-inch pieces and combine in a mixing bowl with the flour, cumin, salt, and sugar. Using the paddle attachment, mix on low speed until the butter is broken into bits and the mixture is crumbly. Add the ice water and pulse the mixer a few times. Turn the dough out onto a work surface and work it together with your hands. Wrap in plastic wrap and chill in the refrigerator for at least 20 minutes.

Preheat oven to 375°F. On a well-floured work surface, roll the dough to 1/8 inch thick. Dust with flour as necessary to keep the dough manageable and prevent it from sticking. Prepare an 8- or 10-inch tart pan by greasing with butter or oil and dusting with flour, tapping out any excess. Transfer the dough to the pan by rolling it onto the rolling pin, then out into the pan. Carefully press the dough into the bottom of the pan and around the sides. You can cut off excess overhanging dough by rolling the pin over the top of the shell. Place a large piece of aluminum foil inside the tart shell and fill with pie weights or other dry weights, such as dried beans or rice. This will prevent the dough from bubbling as it "blind bakes." Bake for 12 to 14 minutes. Remove the foil and weights and brush the inside of the tart shell with egg white in order to seal it. Return to the oven and bake for another 3 minutes. Remove and allow to cool. Reduce the oven temperature to 325°F.

To prepare the filling, cut each avocado in half lengthwise and remove the pit. Scoop the flesh out of the skin into a food processor with the lime juice and eggs. Puree for 30 seconds, or until smooth. Transfer to a bowl and whisk in the cream, milk, salt, nutmeg, and allspice. Pour the filling into the tart shell and bake for 30 to 35 minutes, until the filling is well set. Lightly tap the side of the pan. If the custard ripples in the center, continue baking until it is firm. Remove and allow to cool before serving.

Avocado Tart

Tangerine Tart

Sweet tangerines are one of my favorite citrus fruits and have always been a source of inspiration for creating wonderful desserts. This delicious tart is quick and simple, and makes a refreshing and versatile end to lunch or dinner or a good midafternoon snack with tea. You can make a low-fat version by using plain low-fat yogurt instead of sour cream for the custard. For a richer dessert, top with a scoop of Cardamom Brittle Ice Cream (page 22).

For the crust

1/2 cup (1 stick) unsalted butter

1 1/4 cups all-purpose flour

1/2 teaspoon ground cloves

1/4 teaspoon salt

1 teaspoon sugar

1/4 cup ice water

For the filling

1 cup orange juice

3/4 cup sour cream or plain yogurt

1/4 cup brown sugar

1/2 teaspoon vanilla

1/2 teaspoon ground cloves

1/4 teaspoon finely ground black pepper (optional)

8 to 10 tangerines, preferably seedless, such as Clementines

Cut the butter into 1/2-inch pieces and combine in a mixing bowl with the flour, cloves, salt, and sugar. Using the paddle attachment, mix on low speed until the butter is broken into bits and the mixture is crumbly. Add the ice water and pulse the mixer a few times. Turn the dough out onto a work surface and work it together with your hands. Wrap in plastic wrap and chill in the refrigerator for at least 20 minutes.

Preheat oven to 375°F. On a well-floured work surface, roll the dough to 1/8 inch thick. Dust with flour as necessary to keep the dough manageable and prevent it from sticking. Prepare an 8- or 10-inch tart pan by greasing with butter or oil and dusting with flour, tapping out any excess. Transfer the dough to the pan by rolling it onto the rolling pin, then out into the pan. Carefully press the dough into the bottom of the pan and around the sides. You can cut off excess overhanging dough by rolling the pin over the top of the shell. Place a large piece of aluminum foil inside the tart shell and fill with pie weights or other dry weights, such as dried beans or rice. This will prevent the dough from bubbling as it "blind bakes." Bake for 12 to 14 minutes. Remove the foil and weights and brush the inside of the tart shell with egg white in order to seal it. Return to the oven and bake for another 3 minutes. Remove and allow to cool.

For the filling, place the orange juice in a saucepan over medium heat and simmer for 12 to 14 minutes, until it has reduced to approximately 1/4 cup. Meanwhile, whisk the sour cream or yogurt together with the brown sugar, vanilla, cloves, and black pepper. Turn this custard into the baked tart shell and spread evenly with a spatula. Peel the tangerines and separate the sections. Peel off any stringy, bitter white pith sticking to the sections. Arrange them in a spiral pattern on top of the tart custard. Brush or spoon the reduced orange juice over the tangerine sections as a glaze. Chill the tart in the refrigerator for at least 20 minutes before serving.

Tangerine Tart with Cardamom Ice Cream

Guava Crème Brûlée

MAKES *6* TO *8* INDIVIDUAL BRÛLÉES

Crème brûlées were the darlings of restaurant desserts in the 1980s, served extensively in restaurants around the United States. Usually flavored with more traditional North American fruits, the rich crème brûlée is nicely balanced by the citrus, floral flavors of the guava. Guavas are a popular fruit throughout much of Latin America, especially in Cuba, Puerto Rico, and Mexico. This delicate dessert draws from these Latin influences, showcasing the luscious guavas.

4 egg yolks

1/4 cup sugar

2¹/2 cups heavy cream

4 guavas

2 tablespoons sugar

Preheat oven to 300°F. In a bowl, whisk the yolks and sugar together until smooth and the color is lightened. Bring the cream to a simmer in saucepan over medium heat. Pour the cream into the yolk mixture while whisking. Set aside.

Peel the guavas and roughly chop the flesh. Puree in a food processor until smooth. Pass the puree through a fine strainer to remove the seeds, then whisk it into the custard. Divide the guava custard among six to eight 4-ounce porcelain ramekins and place on a pan with 1-inch sides that is half-filled with water. This water bath will ensure gentle baking of the custard. Bake for 35 to 40 minutes. Lightly tap the sides of the ramekins. If the custard ripples in the center, continue baking until firm. Remove from oven and chill the custards thoroughly in the refrigerator for at least 1 hour.

When ready to serve, sprinkle the tops of the custards with an even layer of sugar. Place under a broiler to melt and caramelize, watching attentively so they don't burn. Serve immediately.

Satsuma Mandarin–Vanilla Crème Brûlée

As a child growing up in New England, I thought mandarin orange sections came only from a can. I didn't taste fresh mandarin oranges until I was much older. Needless to say, they're much more delicious! In this recipe, the tender, tiny sections of Satsuma mandarins are baked into vanilla-flavored crème brûlée—an exquisite contrast between bright citrus flavors and the rich creamy vanilla custard.

4 egg yolks

1/4 cup sugar

2 1/2 cups heavy cream

1 vanilla bean, split and scraped, or 1 teaspoon vanilla extract

4 Satsuma mandarins (or 4 tangerines or 2 oranges)

2 tablespoons sugar

Preheat oven to 300°F. In a bowl, whisk the yolks and sugar together until smooth and the color is lightened. Bring the cream and vanilla bean or extract to a simmer in a saucepan over medium heat. Pour the cream into the yolk mixture while whisking. Set aside.

Peel the tangerines and separate the sections. Peel off any stringy, bitter white pith sticking to the sections. Divide the sections among six to eight 4-ounce porcelain ramekins, laying them on the bottom. Pour the custard on top of the tangerines, filling the ramekins. Place them on a pan with 1-inch sides that is half-filled with water. This water bath will ensure gentle baking of the custard. Bake for 35 to 40 minutes. Lightly tap the sides of the ramekins. If the custard ripples in the center, continue baking until firm. Remove from oven and chill the custards thoroughly in the refrigerator, for at least 1 hour.

When ready to serve, sprinkle the tops of the custards with an even layer of sugar. Place them under a broiler to melt and caramelize, watching attentively so they don't burn. Serve immediately.

Spiced Natilla with Blood Orange

Natillas are a traditional spiced custard of Latin cuisines in the southwestern United States and Central America. This version, which we serve at the Coyote Cafe, adds a modern twist to this custard that has an old history in many New Mexican Hispanic families. If you can't find blood oranges, which add vibrant color to the custard, you can use regular sweet oranges. If desired, serve with Nutmeg-Orange Cookies (page 135) or Aniseed Cookies (page 138).

3/4 cup milk

2 teaspoons unflavored gelatin

1 1/4 cups heavy cream

**1 vanilla bean, split and scraped, or 1 1/2 teaspoons
      vanilla extract**

1/2 teaspoon ground nutmeg

1/2 teaspoon ground allspice

1/4 cup brown sugar

4 blood oranges, or regular oranges

Pour the milk into a saucepan and sprinkle the gelatin on top of it. Allow to sit for 2 minutes to allow the gelatin to "bloom." Add the cream, vanilla, spices, and sugar and bring to a simmer over medium heat. Pass the mixture through a fine strainer.

Using a sharp chef's knife, trim the tops and bottoms off the oranges, then cut all the peel and pith from the inner flesh, working your way around the fruit. Section the oranges by cutting between each membrane and removing each wedge of fruit. Divide the orange sections among 6 to 8 goblets or bowls and pour the custard over them, or line the bottoms of 6 timbale molds with the blood orange segments, fill them with the custard, chill them for 1 hour, then dip the molds in warm water and unmold onto plates. Chill in the refrigerator for at least 1 hour before serving.

Spiced Natilla with Blood Orange

Jamaican Red Papaya–Vanilla Pudding

One day while enjoying a sweet, ripe papaya, I was struck by its rich and smooth puddinglike quality, inspiring me to create a papaya pudding. When Donna and I lived in West Africa, we ate fresh papayas for breakfast and dessert when they were in season, never getting enough of their fragrant flavors. If you can't find Jamaican red papayas, any variety would do for this pudding.

2 eggs

2 egg yolks

1/2 cup sugar

1 1/2 cups heavy cream

1/4 cup milk

1 vanilla bean, split and scraped, or 1 teaspoon vanilla extract

1 Jamaican red papaya, or other papaya

Juice of 1 lime

Whisk the eggs, yolks, and sugar together in a bowl until lightened in color. Combine the cream, milk, and vanilla bean or extract in a saucepan and put over medium heat. As soon as it comes to a simmer, remove from the heat and pass through a fine strainer. Pour the cream mixture into the eggs while whisking. Set aside to cool.

Preheat oven to 300°F. Peel the papayas, scoop out the seeds, and roughly chop the flesh. Puree the fruit in a food processor with the lime juice until smooth. Whisk the puree into the custard mixture, and divide between six to eight 4-ounce ramekins. Place them on a pan with 1-inch sides that is half-filled with water. This water bath will ensure gentle baking of the custard. Bake for 35 to 40 minutes. Lightly tap the sides of the ramekins. If the custard ripples in the center, continue baking until firm. Remove from oven and chill the puddings thoroughly in the refrigerator for at least 1 hour before serving.

Warm Desserts

Some of the strongest, most intense and immediate flavors of tropical fruits can be best experienced through warm preparations. Simple, warm desserts draw out the brightest flavors of most tropical fruits, including bananas, mangoes, pineapples, citrus, coconuts, and guavas. The pungent flavors of tropical spices also reach heightened tones and clarity when added to baked goods or briefly heated with fruits and served in warm compotes, custards, and sauces. Allspice, cardamom, cinnamon, and ginger all add different complexities to tropical fruits and nuts, and can transform a good dessert into an exceptional and unforgettable dessert experience.

Although some of these recipes may seem unusual in their ingredients and flavor combinations, you'll find the preparations are based on familiar American and European home-style desserts and baked goods. Common cakes and puddings can be transformed into new and exciting desserts with the simple addition of tropical and subtropical ingredients. Add green mangoes to an apple pie, serve pancakes with pineapples instead of blueberries, make a fruit crisp with papayas and coconuts, or bake whole Asian pears instead of apples. Other preparations in this chapter are a little less common, but no more difficult. Infuse a light broth with bananas for a unique sweet dessert soup, or grill some spiced bananas for a delicious and unusual treat reminiscent of fire-roasted preparations popular in the Caribbean.

Desserts don't need to be complicated to be satisfying and fulfilling. When I first began to experiment with tropical fruits, I made simple warm compotes that take no more than a few minutes to cook and serve, like chunks of pineapple, papaya, and mango lightly simmered in a syrup flavored with vanilla and muscat wine just until the fruits are warmed all the way through. I always like to top a tropical fruit compote with a scoop of ice cream for a refreshing temperature contrast, as the ice cream melts decadently into the warm fruits and pleases the palate with its invigorating sweet chill. The most humble and basic ingredients, such as bananas, oranges, or vanilla, can be the starting point for warm, exotic, and seductive simple desserts.

Clear Banana-Caramel Soup with Pineapple Dumpling

MAKES *6* TO *8* SERVINGS

Clear soups are my sweet interpretations of consommés, light and flavorful warm broths. They make a clean and elegant finish to a meal in summer or winter. This one gets its rich banana essence by steeping the banana peels to extract their flavor, and is topped with fresh banana and a sweet pineapple dumpling. I think banana, caramel, and pineapple are flavors made for each other—you can never go wrong with this combination!

For the soup

1/4 cup sugar

3 cups water

2 bananas

For the pineapple dumplings

1/2 pineapple

2 tablespoons brown sugar

1 tablespoon dark rum or vanilla extract

1/2 sheet puff pastry

1 egg, beaten lightly

To make the soup, sprinkle the sugar in a sauté pan and place over medium heat. Allow it to melt and caramelize. When it is amber brown and lightly smoking, tip the pan back and forth to mix the lighter caramel on the edges with the darker caramel in the center. Carefully stir in 1/2 cup of water with a whisk, taking caution because it may splatter. Add the remaining water and turn off the heat.

Wash the bananas, peel and reserve the skins. Roughly chop the bananas into 1/4- to 1/2-inch chunks and divide into two piles. Add one-half of the bananas and the skins to the caramel water and bring to a steady simmer over low heat for 25 minutes. Pass the banana caramel soup through a fine strainer and reserve for later.

To prepare the pineapple dumplings, using a sharp chef's knife, trim the top and bottom off the half pineapple and then slice off the skin. Cut in half lengthwise from top to bottom. Trim the core from each piece and cut the fruit into 1/2-inch chunks.

Combine the pineapple, brown sugar, and rum or vanilla in a saucepan over medium heat. Cook over low heat for 20 minutes, stirring periodically, until the pineapple browns and cooks down. Remove from heat and cool mixture thoroughly in the refrigerator.

Preheat oven to 400°F. Cut the puff pastry into six to eight 3-inch squares. Brush some of the beaten egg on two adjoining edges of each square, and spoon 1 tablespoon of the cooled pineapple mixture into the center of each square. Fold the egg-washed pastry edges over to their opposite edges, creating a triangle shape, and press firmly with a fork to seal them together. Place on a nonstick cookie sheet, or one that has been brushed lightly with oil. Brush the tops of the pastries with egg wash and bake for 14 to 16 minutes, until the pastry is deep amber brown. Remove from oven.

While the dumplings are still warm, place the soup in a saucepan over medium heat. When it is very warm, divide between 6 to 8 bowls, place a spoonful of the reserved chopped banana in the center of each, and top the fresh banana with a pineapple dumpling.

> *Bananas ripe and green, and ginger root,*
> *Cocoa in pods and alligator pears,*
> *And tangerines and mangoes and grape fruit,*
> *Fit for the highest prize at parish fairs.*
> —CLAUDE MCKAY, FROM "THE TROPICS IN NEW YORK"

Clear Banana-Caramel Soup with Pineapple Dumpling

Clear Lemongrass Soup with Candied Kumquat and Cherimoya

*Makes **6** to **8** servings*

In West Africa, we frequently brewed tea from the strawlike blades of wild lemongrass that friends brought to us from their farms. This recipe calls for the stalks of the plant, which have a bright, lemony flavor. Its aromatic character makes a refreshing clear soup, accented by the sweet orange punch of candied kumquats and the pungent, musty spice of fresh cherimoya. For a richer dessert, top each bowl of soup with a scoop of Pineapple Sorbet (page 10), Roasted Banana Sorbet (page 17), or Double Vanilla Ice Cream (page 21).

For the soup

4 lemongrass stalks

3 cups water

2 tablespoons sugar

1 tablespoon honey

For the fruits

8 to 10 kumquats

2 cups water

1/2 cup sugar

1 cherimoya

To make the soup, slice the lemongrass stalks crosswise into 1/2-inch pieces. Combine them in a saucepan with the water, sugar, and honey and place over medium heat. Bring the mixture to a boil, then reduce the heat to low and simmer for 20 minutes. Turn off the heat and allow the lemongrass to steep in the liquid for 1 hour. Strain and return to the saucepan.

To prepare the fruits, cut the kumquats into 1/16-inch-thick slices. Combine in a saucepan with 1 1/4 cups of the water and place over medium heat. Bring to a boil, reduce heat to low, and simmer for 20 minutes. Drain the water, and add the remaining 3/4 cup water and sugar to the pot with the kumquat slices. Return to medium heat and bring to boil, reduce heat to low, and simmer another 20 minutes. The kumquat slices should be translucent and candied. Remove from heat, and leave the kumquats in the syrup until ready to serve. They can be kept covered in the refrigerator for up to 2 weeks.

Using a sharp paring knife, peel the skin from the cherimoya and cut the fruit into 1-inch chunks or wedges. Pull the black pits out of the pieces of fruit and discard.

When ready to serve, warm the lemongrass soup over medium heat. Divide among 6 to 8 bowls, and sprinkle with the candied kumquat slices and cherimoya chunks. Serve immediately.

*MAKES **6** TO **8** SERVINGS*

Coconut and guava make an incredible rich flavor combination, tempered in this recipe by the citrusy bite of fresh grapefruit and orange. For a double coconut whammy, use the extra coconut meat to make a batch of Coconut Ice Cream (page 18) to serve with the soup.

2 coconuts

2 guavas or 2 feijoas

1/4 cup sugar

2 oranges

1 grapefruit

Preheat oven to 400°F. Poke the "eyes" of both coconuts with a blunt tool, like a screwdriver. Drain the coconut water through a strainer into a saucepan. Place one of the coconuts in the oven and roast for 20 minutes. (Reserve the other coconut for another use.) Remove it from the oven and decrease the temperature to 350°F. Allow the coconut to cool, then crack it open and remove the white flesh by prying it out with a spoon. Use a peeler to make 1 cup of coconut shavings. Spread the shavings on a dry cookie sheet and roast in the oven for 12 to 14 minutes.

Cut the guavas into 4 slices and combine in a saucepan with the coconut water and sugar. Place over low heat and bring to a simmer. Simmer for 10 minutes, then turn the heat off and allow the guavas to steep in the mixture for at least 1/2 hour.

Using a sharp chef's knife, trim the tops and bottoms off the citrus fruits, then cut all the peel and pith from the inner flesh, working your way around the fruit. Section the oranges and grapefruit by cutting between each membrane and removing each wedge of fruit. Set aside until ready to serve.

Pass the coconut water–guava mixture through a fine strainer into a saucepan, using a spoon or ladle to push the softened guava pulp through the strainer. Place over medium heat until the mixture is very warm. Divide the soup among 6 to 8 bowls. Scatter citrus sections into each bowl and sprinkle the roasted coconut shavings into the centers.

Passion Fruit Soufflé

MAKES **6** TO **8** SOUFFLÉS

The fragrant, acidic pulp of passion fruits makes an exquisitely delicious soufflé. Like lemons, passion fruits are refreshing and palate cleansing, and their floral, citrus intensity is particularly suited to making soufflés. This is an elegant and unique dessert for a perfect ending to a special meal.

1/2 cup milk

2 eggs, separated

1/4 cup plus 1 tablespoon sugar

2 tablespoons all-purpose flour

4 passion fruits

Preheat oven to 400°F. Place the milk in a saucepan over medium heat and bring to a boil. In a bowl, whisk the egg yolks with 1/4 cup of the sugar until lightened in color. Whisk in the flour until well combined. Pour the heated milk into the yolk mixture while whisking, and continue whisking until well combined. Return the mixture to the saucepan and place over medium heat. Stir constantly as the pastry cream thickens and begins to bubble, and continue stirring while it boils for 10 to 15 seconds. Remove from heat and set aside.

Cut the passion fruits in half and use a spoon to scoop out all the pulp into a blender. Pulse a few times to separate the pulp from the seeds, then pass the mixture through a fine strainer, pressing the pulp with a spoon or ladle to remove as much juice as possible. Stir the passion fruit juice into the pastry cream mixture.

Prepare six to eight 4-ounce ceramic ramekins or soufflé dishes by brushing with melted butter or oil and dusting with sugar, tapping out any excess. Using a mixer, whip the egg whites to soft peaks while sprinkling in the remaining 1 tablespoon sugar. Gently fold the whipped egg whites into the passion fruit pastry cream, taking care not to stir them too much and deflate the air from the whites.

Divide among the prepared soufflé dishes, which should be filled to just over the edges. Using a metal spatula, scrape over the top edges of the dishes to level the tops of the soufflés. Place in a pan with 1-inch sides that is filled with 1/2 inch water. This "water bath" will ensure gentle baking of the soufflés. Bake for 16 to 18 minutes, or until the soufflés have risen about 1/2 inch above the rims of the dishes. Remove from oven and serve immediately.

Passion Fruit Soufflé

Meyer Lemon Soufflé

Makes 6 to 8 soufflés

Meyer lemons are slightly sweeter and have a fuller flavor than common lemons, so they are worth seeking out for this elegant, light dessert. But if you can't find them, regular lemons will also achieve delicious results.

1/2 cup milk

2 eggs, separated

5 tablespoons sugar

2 tablespoons all-purpose flour

2 to 3 Meyer lemons

Preheat oven to 400°F. Place the milk in a saucepan over medium heat and bring to a boil. In a bowl, whisk the egg yolks with 4 tablespoons of the sugar until lightened. Whisk in the flour until well combined. Pour the heated milk into the yolk mixture while whisking, and continue whisking until well combined. Return the mixture to the saucepan over medium heat. Stir constantly as the pastry cream thickens and begins to bubble, and continue stirring while it boils for 10 to 15 seconds. Set aside.

Remove the zest from the one of the lemons with a zester or peeler. Mince the zest with a chef's knife. Cut the lemons in half and squeeze their juice through a strainer. Add the minced zest to the juice. Stir the lemon juice and zest into the pastry cream.

Prepare six to eight 4-ounce soufflé dishes by brushing with melted butter or oil and dusting with sugar. Using a mixer, whip the egg whites to soft peaks while sprinkling in the remaining 1 tablespoon sugar. Gently fold the whipped egg whites into the lemon pastry cream, taking care not to stir them too much and deflate the air from the whites.

Divide among the prepared soufflé dishes, which should be filled to just over the edges. Using a metal spatula, scrape over the top edges of the dishes to level the tops of the soufflés. Place in a pan with 1-inch sides that is filled with 1/2 inch water. This "water bath" will ensure gentle baking of the soufflés. Bake for 16 to 18 minutes, or until the soufflés have risen about 1/2 inch above the rims of the dishes. Remove from oven and serve immediately.

Chocolate–Roasted Almond Soufflé

MAKES *6* TO *8* SOUFFLÉS

This soufflé is soul-satisfying for any chocolate-lover. Who can resist this rich, dark chocolate dessert studded with earthy tones of roasted almonds? I love chocolate soufflés for their paradoxical nature—their light, airy texture delivers a surprisingly deep, strong chocolate flavor.

1/2 cup almonds

3/4 cup milk

2 eggs, separated

6 tablespoons sugar

1 teaspoon cocoa powder

2 tablespoons all-purpose flour

2 ounces bittersweet chocolate, finely chopped

Preheat oven to 375°F. Spread the almonds on a dry cookie sheet and roast in the oven for 16 to 18 minutes. Remove from oven, and increase the temperature to 400°F. Grind the nuts finely in a food processor. Set aside.

Place the milk in a saucepan over medium heat and bring to a boil. In a bowl, whisk the egg yolks with 4 tablespoons of the sugar until lightened in color. Whisk in the cocoa powder and flour until well combined. Pour the heated milk into the yolk mixture while whisking, and continue whisking until well combined. Return the mixture to the saucepan and place over medium heat. Stir constantly as the pastry cream thickens and begins to bubble, and continue stirring while it boils for 10 to 15 seconds. Remove from heat and stir in the chopped chocolate and ground almonds. Set aside.

Prepare six to eight 4-ounce ceramic ramekins or soufflé dishes by brushing with melted butter or oil and dusting with sugar, tapping out any excess. Using a mixer, whip the egg whites to soft peaks while sprinkling in the remaining 2 tablespoons sugar. Gently fold the whipped egg whites into the chocolate almond pastry cream, taking care not to stir them too much and deflate the air from the whites.

Divide among the prepared soufflé dishes, which should be filled to just over the edges. Using a metal spatula, scrape over the top edges of the dishes to level the tops of the soufflés. Place in a pan with 1-inch sides that is filled with 1/2 inch water. This "water bath" will ensure gentle baking of the soufflés. Bake for 16 to 18 minutes, or until the soufflés have risen about 1/2 inch above the rims of the dishes. Remove from oven and serve immediately.

It was inevitable: the scent of bitter almonds always reminded him of the fate of unrequited love.
—GABRIEL GARCÍA MARQUEZ,
LOVE IN THE TIME OF CHOLERA

Key Lime Custard Cakes

MAKES *6* TO *8* SERVINGS

Key limes are the most flavorful variety of this green citrus, and are most familiar to us in the form of key lime pies. They are produced extensively in the Florida Keys, from whence they get their name. They are slightly sweeter than other limes, with a distinctive, full flavor. These custard cakes are a superlight, vibrant version of the more traditional Key Lime Pie. If you can't find key limes, substitute the common limes.

2 tablespoons unsalted butter

3/4 cup plus 2 tablespoons sugar

1/8 teaspoon salt

4 eggs, separated

6 tablespoons all-purpose flour

Juice of 4 to 5 key limes (or substitute common regular limes, approximately 1/2 cup juice)

1/2 cup milk

1/2 cup heavy cream

Preheat oven to 400°F. Combine the butter and 3/4 cup of the sugar in a mixing bowl and whip at high speed. Add the salt and 3 egg yolks one at a time and whip for 2 minutes until lightened in color. Reserve the remaining egg yolk for another recipe or discard. Reduce speed to low, add the flour, and mix until well combined. Add the lime juice and mix until smooth. Add the milk and cream and mix until smooth.

In a separate mixing bowl, whip the 4 egg whites to soft peaks while sprinkling in the remaining 2 tablespoons sugar. Gently fold the whipped egg whites into the lime batter, taking care not to stir too much and deflate the air from the whites.

Prepare six to eight 4-ounce ceramic ramekins or soufflé dishes by brushing with melted butter or oil and dusting with sugar, tapping out any excess. Divide the batter among the prepared soufflé dishes, which should be filled to the edges. Using a metal spatula, scrape over the top edges of the dishes to level the tops of the custard cakes. Place in a pan with 1-inch sides that is filled with 1/2 inch water. This "water bath" will ensure gentle baking of the cakes. Bake for 14 to 16 minutes, or until the cakes have risen about 1/2 inch above the rims of the dishes. Remove from oven and serve while still warm. The custard cakes may be served in the ceramic dishes or inverted onto plates served with tropical fruits or sorbet.

Key Lime Custard Cake

Lemon Angel Cake with Caramel Sauce

MAKES ONE 8- TO 10-INCH ANGEL CAKE, OR 8 TO 10 SERVINGS

Light, spongy angel food cake has long been a favorite American dessert. In this recipe, the simple cake is brightened with refreshing lemon zip and topped with a rich, caramel sauce. One bite of this sweet-and-sour combination inspires celestial bliss to rival the angels! Serve it with a heavenly scoop of Double Vanilla Ice Cream (page 21) or topped with segments of orange and grapefruit.

For the angel cake

2 lemons

7 egg whites

3/4 cup sugar

3/4 cup all-purpose flour

For the caramel sauce

1/2 cup sugar

1/2 cup heavy cream

To make the cake, preheat oven to 325°F. Remove the zest from the lemons with a zester or peeler and chop it finely with a chef's knife. Juice the lemons through a strainer to remove any seeds. Add the zest to the juice and set aside.

Whip the egg whites in a mixer on high speed until soft, frothy peaks form. Sprinkle in one-half of the sugar and continue whipping to stiff peaks. Stir together the flour and remaining sugar. Sift one-third of this dry mixture over the whipped whites and gently fold together. Pour in one-third of the lemon juice and gently fold. Continue alternating adding the dry mixture and lemon juice to the whites until all ingredients are combined and the mixture is smooth.

Prepare an 8- to 10-inch tube pan or bundt cake pan by brushing with oil or melted butter and dusting with flour, tapping out any excess. Pour the batter into the pan and bake for 1 hour, or until cake springs back when lightly touched. Cool in the pan.

You can prepare the sauce while the cake is baking or cooling. Sprinkle the sugar into a sauté pan and place over medium heat. Allow sugar to melt and begin to brown. When it is caramelized and lightly smoking, carefully add the cream and stir to dissolve all the caramel. If it clumps up a bit, continue to stir over the heat until smooth. Set aside. When ready to serve, cut the cake into slices. Place them on a cookie sheet and warm them in the oven at 375°F for 6 to 8 minutes before transferring them to individual plates. Reheat the caramel sauce in a saucepan over medium heat, drizzle each piece with caramel sauce, and serve immediately.

Lemon Angel Cake with Caramel Sauce

Bitter Orange Custard Cakes

MAKES *6* TO *8* SERVINGS

Seville bitter oranges are too sour to eat fresh, but have a fantastic, tart flavor for cooking and baking. In this recipe, I use them to liven up custard cakes, a classic old-fashioned American dessert. During its short baking time, a pleasing layer of warm custard forms on the bottom of this soufflé-like cake. If you can't find bitter oranges, you can substitute grapefruits for a close variation.

2 tablespoons unsalted butter

3/4 cup plus 2 tablespoons sugar

1/8 teaspoon salt

4 eggs, separated

6 tablespoons all-purpose flour

Juice of 2 Seville bitter oranges (or substitute 1 grapefruit, approximately 1/2 cup juice)

1/2 cup milk

1/2 cup heavy cream

Preheat oven to 400°F. Combine the butter and 3/4 cup of the sugar in a mixing bowl and whip at high speed. Add the salt and 3 egg yolks one at a time and whip for 2 minutes until lightened in color. Reserve the fourth egg yolk for another recipe or discard. Reduce speed to low, add the flour, and mix until well combined. Add the citrus juice and mix until smooth. Add the milk and cream and mix until smooth.

In a separate mixing bowl, whip the 4 egg whites to soft peaks while sprinkling in the remaining 2 tablespoons sugar. Gently fold the whipped egg whites into the citrus batter, taking care not to stir too much and deflate the air from the whites.

Prepare six to eight 4-ounce ceramic ramekins or soufflé dishes by brushing with melted butter or oil and dusting with sugar, tapping out any excess. Divide the batter among the prepared soufflé dishes, which should be filled just to the edges. Using a metal spatula, scrape over the top edges of the dishes to level the tops of the custard cakes. Place in a pan with 1-inch sides that is filled with 1/2 inch water. This "water bath" will ensure gentle baking of the cakes. Bake for 14 to 16 minutes, or until the cakes have risen about 1/2" above the rims of the dishes. Remove from oven and serve while still warm. The custard cakes may be served in the ceramic dishes or inverted onto plates served with tropical fruits or sorbet.

Cinnamon Red-Hot Angel Cake with Chocolate Sauce

MAKES ONE 8- TO 10-INCH ANGEL CAKE, OR **8** TO **10** SERVINGS

Like the ancient Aztecs did, contemporary Mayans in Central America often spice their chocolate drinks with hot red chiles. This recipe draws influences from their chile-flavored chocolate, and is also reminiscent of those small, round cinnamon red-hot candies we all loved as children. The light angel cake is spiced with cinnamon and cayenne pepper, and served with a rich bittersweet chocolate sauce. This heavenly chocolate dessert isn't "food of the gods"—it's food of the angels!

For the angel cake

7 egg whites

1/2 teaspoon lemon juice

3/4 cup sugar

3/4 cup all-purpose flour

2 teaspoons ground cinnamon

1 teaspoon ground cayenne pepper

For the chocolate sauce

6 ounces (about 1 1/2 cups chopped) bittersweet chocolate, melted

1/2 cup hot water

To make the cake, preheat oven to 325°F. Combine the egg whites and lemon juice in a mixer and whip at high speed to soft peaks. Continue whipping while sprinkling in half of the sugar, and whip to stiff peaks. Set aside.

Stir together the remaining sugar, flour, cinnamon, and cayenne pepper. Sift half of this dry mixture over the whipped egg whites, and gently fold together with a rubber spatula. Sift in the remaining dry mixture and fold until well combined.

Prepare an 8- to 10-inch tube pan or bundt cake pan by brushing with oil or melted butter and dusting with flour, tapping out any excess. Pour the batter into the pan and bake for 1 hour, or until cake springs back when lightly touched. Cool in the pan.

You can prepare the sauce while the cake is baking or cooling. Whisk together the melted chocolate and hot water until smooth. Set aside. When ready to serve, cut the cake into slices. Place them on a cookie sheet and warm them in the oven at 375°F for 6 to 8 minutes before transferring them to individual plates. Drizzle with chocolate sauce and serve.

These two settlements of Cavit and Subanin [in the Spice Islands] produce the best cinnamon that can be found. And we remained there two days, and loaded our ships with it. . . . This cinnamon tree is no taller than three or four cubits, and as thick as the finger of a hand, and it has no more than three or four branches, and its leaf is like that of the laurel, and its bark is the cinnamon, which is gathered twice a year. So the wood grows strongly and the leaves when green smell like the cinnamon. And they call it Caiumana. Caiu means wood and mana means sweet, hence sweet wood.

—ANTONIO PIGAFETTA, *MAGELLAN'S VOYAGE*

Warm Vanilla-Bean Cake with Papaya and Cashews

MAKES ONE 10-INCH ROUND CAKE, OR **8** TO **10** SERVINGS, OR **8** TO **10** INDIVIDUAL CAKES

This warm, simple cake is filled with fresh, intense vanilla flavor. Topped with sweet papaya and roasted cashews, it makes a simple ending to an evening meal, luncheon, or special celebration. Serve it with a scoop of Double Vanilla Ice Cream (page 21). If desired, use 8 to 10 small ceramic baking dishes (ramekins) to make individual cakes.

11/2 **cups cashews**

1/2 **cup milk**

3 **vanilla beans, split and scraped**

1 **teaspoon vanilla extract**

1/2 **cup (1 stick) unsalted butter, softened**

11/2 **cups sugar**

3/4 **cup honey**

2 **eggs**

2 **cups all-purpose flour**

1/4 **teaspoon baking soda**

1/2 **teaspoon salt**

1 **medium papaya**

Preheat oven to 375°F. Spread the cashews on a dry cookie sheet and roast in the oven for 12 to 14 minutes, until golden brown. Remove from oven and set aside. Do not turn the oven off.

Combine the milk, vanilla beans, and vanilla extract in a saucepan and bring to a simmer over medium heat. Remove from heat and place in the refrigerator until cool to the touch.

In a large bowl, using a mixer, cream the butter, sugar, and honey for 5 minutes, or until light and fluffy. Add the eggs one at a time and continue whipping until smooth. Remove the cooled milk from the refrigerator and pick out the vanilla pods. Add the milk to the creamed butter and eggs, and mix until smooth.

In a bowl, sift together the flour, baking soda, and salt. Gently fold half of these dry ingredients into the wet mixture until combined, then fold in the remaining dry ingredients until entire batter is smooth.

Prepare a 10-inch round cake pan (or the ramekins) by brushing with oil or melted butter and dusting with flour, tapping out any excess. Pour the batter into the pan and bake for 18 to 20 minutes, or until a paring knife inserted into the center comes out clean. If making individual cakes, bake for 16 to 18 minutes. Allow to cool on a rack.

Peel and halve the papaya and scoop out the seeds. Place the halves flat on a cutting surface and thinly slice them lengthwise. Set aside until ready to serve.

When ready to serve, cut the cake into slices and place them on a cookie sheet. Warm in the oven at 375°F for 6 to 8 minutes, then transfer to individual plates. Top each piece of cake with slices of papaya and sprinkle with roasted cashews.

Warm Vanilla-Bean Cake with Papaya and Cashews

Pineapple Spice Cake

MAKES ONE 10-INCH ROUND CAKE, OR **8** TO **10** SERVINGS, OR **8** TO **10** INDIVIDUAL CAKES

In this recipe, slices of pineapple are baked inside a delicious cake flavored with hints of cinnamon, nutmeg, ginger, allspice, and rich, roasted Brazil nuts. When topped with Tropical Nut Brittle Ice Cream (page 21), you have a dessert bursting with the fruits, spices, and nuts of the tropics!

1 cup Brazil nuts

1 cup (2 sticks) unsalted butter

1 tablespoon honey

1 cup sugar

1/2 teaspoon ground cinnamon

1/2 teaspoon ground nutmeg

1/2 teaspoon ground ginger

1/2 teaspoon ground allspice

1/2 teaspoon finely ground black pepper

1/2 teaspoon salt

1/2 teaspoon baking soda

1 cup all-purpose flour

6 egg whites

1 pineapple

Preheat oven to 375°F. Spread the Brazil nuts on a dry cookie sheet and roast in the oven for 12 to 14 minutes, until golden brown. Remove from oven and allow to briefly cool. Place the roasted nuts in a food processor and pulverize until medium ground. Set aside.

Place the butter in a large saucepan over medium heat. Allow to melt and continue cooking until lightly browned. When the browned butter is lightly smoking and emits a nutty scent, turn off the heat and stir in the honey. In a separate bowl, stir together the ground Brazil nuts, sugar, spices, salt, baking soda, and flour. Stir the browned butter into the dry mixture.

Whip the egg whites in a mixer until soft, frothy peaks form. Fold the whites into the butter-flour mixture until smooth.

Using a sharp chef's knife, trim the top and bottom off the pineapple and then slice off the skin, working your way around the fruit. Cut in quarters lengthwise from top to bottom. Trim the core from each piece and slice the quarters lengthwise into 1/8-inch-thick slices. Prepare a 10-inch round cake pan (or individual pans) by brushing with oil or melted butter and dusting with flour, tapping out any excess. Lay the pineapple slices in the bottom of the pan, fanning them into a spiral or shingled pattern. Pour the spiced batter over them. Bake in the oven for 35 to 40 minutes (or 25 to 30 minutes for individual cakes), until the cake springs back when lightly touched or a knife inserted into the center comes out clean. Allow to cool on a rack.

When ready to serve, cut the cake into slices and place them on a cookie sheet. Warm in the oven at 375°F for 6 to 8 minutes, then transfer to individual plates and serve.

Pineapple Spice Cake with Tropical Nut Brittle Ice Cream

Bittersweet Chocolate Cake

*MAKES ONE 10-INCH ROUND CAKE, OR **8** TO **10** SERVINGS, OR **8** TO **10** INDIVIDUAL CAKES*

This rich, chocolate cake has very little flour in it so its intense chocolate flavor is sure to satisfy even the most discriminating chocolate lover. Use strong, freshly brewed coffee for a rich hint of mocha in the cake. It pairs especially well with the Roasted Peanut Ice Cream (page 22), which adds an earthy, nutty character to the dessert. You can also serve it with Double Vanilla Ice Cream (page 21) or store-bought vanilla ice cream.

6 ounces bittersweet chocolate, melted

1/2 cup strong brewed coffee

1/2 cup (1 stick) unsalted butter, melted

6 eggs, separated

1/2 cup sugar

1/4 cup all-purpose flour

Preheat oven to 400°F. In a large bowl, whisk together the chocolate, coffee, and melted butter. Set aside.

In another bowl, using a mixer, whip the egg yolks with half of the sugar for 2 minutes, until fluffy and lightened in color. Whisk in the flour until smooth. In a separate mixing bowl, whip the egg whites until soft, frothy peaks form. Add the remaining sugar and continue whipping to stiff peaks.

Whisk the yolk mixture into the chocolate mixture, then gently fold in the egg whites, taking care not to deflate the air in them and reduce the volume.

Prepare 8 individual 4-ounce ceramic ramekins or one 10-inch round cake pan by brushing with oil or melted butter and dusting with flour, tapping out any excess. Bake the small individual cakes for 10 to 12 minutes or the whole round cake for 14 to 16 minutes. Remove from the oven and allow to cool for 5 to 7 minutes, until cool enough to handle but still warm.

Run a paring knife around the edges of the ramekins, and invert the warm cakes onto individual plates. If making a whole cake, invert it onto a cutting surface or serving plate, and slice into individual pieces.

Tamarind Cake with Red Bananas and Caramel Cream

MAKES ONE 10-INCH ROUND CAKE, OR 8 TO 10 SERVINGS, OR 8 TO 10 INDIVIDUAL CAKES

The strong sour and fruity flavor of tamarind injects this simple cake with an unexpected zing that makes it truly unique. Slices of sweet red bananas cooked in a rich, caramel cream perfectly balance with the tart notes of tamarind. Tamarind pulp can be found packaged in specialty stores and some supermarkets, or you can buy the whole pods and scrape out the pulp yourself. Top this cake with scoops of Molasses Ice Cream (page 20) or Roasted Peanut Ice Cream (page 22).

For the cake

1 cup tamarind pulp (5 to 6 pods)

1/2 cup milk

1/2 cup (1 stick) unsalted butter

1 cup brown sugar

1/4 cup molasses

1/4 cup honey

2 eggs

13/4 cups all-purpose flour

1 teaspoon baking soda

1/2 teaspoon salt

1/2 teaspoon ground cinnamon

For the red bananas and caramel cream

5 to 6 red bananas

1/2 cup sugar

1 cup heavy cream

To make the cake, preheat oven to 375°F. Combine the tamarind pulp and milk in a saucepan and place over medium heat. Bring to a simmer while breaking up the tamarind pulp with the edge of a spoon. Stir for several minutes to dissolve the pulp in the warm milk and separate the pits from the pulp. Remove from the heat and pass through a fine strainer, gently pressing the pulp through the strainer with a spoon to squeeze as much tamarind as possible from the fibers and seeds. Place the strained tamarind milk in the refrigerator to cool.

Using a mixer, cream together the butter, brown sugar, molasses, and honey. Add the cooled tamarind milk and whip until well combined, then whip in the eggs one at a time. In a separate bowl, sift together the flour, baking soda, salt, and cinnamon. Fold the dry ingredients into the wet mixture until smooth.

Prepare a 10-inch round cake pan (or the ramekins) by brushing with oil or melted butter and dusting with flour, tapping out any excess. Pour the batter into the pan and bake at 375°F for 18 to 20 minutes (or 16 to 18 minutes for individual cakes), or until a knife inserted into the center comes out clean. Remove from oven and allow to cool in the pan.

Begin preparing the red bananas and caramel cream 10 to 15 minutes before serving the cake. Peel the bananas and slice diagonally into 1/4-inch-thick pieces. Sprinkle the sugar into a sauté pan and place over medium heat. Allow the sugar to melt and begin to brown. When it is amber colored, caramelized, and lightly smoking, gently pour in the cream. The mixture may initially splatter and bubble. Reduce heat to low and stir to dissolve any lumps of caramel. Add the sliced bananas to the caramel cream and cook for 1 minute.

Slice the cake into wedges and place on individual plates. Pour some warm red bananas and caramel cream over each piece and serve immediately.

Warm Baby Banana Cake

*MAKES ONE 10-INCH ROUND CAKE, OR **8** TO **10** SERVINGS, OR **8** TO **10** INDIVIDUAL CAKES*

This cake was inspired by a delicious dessert I had at the famous New York City restaurant Lespinasse, where Gray Kunz is chef. I highly recommend making a batch of Chocolate-Cinnamon Ice Cream (page 18) to serve with this exquisitely spiced banana cake—you will find it well worth the time and effort!

3/4 cup (1 1/2 sticks) unsalted butter

1/2 cup brown sugar

2 tablespoons honey

2 cups pureed baby bananas (6 to 8 whole)

2 eggs

2 cups all-purpose flour

1 cup roasted almonds, coarsely ground

1/2 teaspoon salt

1 teaspoon baking soda

1/2 teaspoon ground cinnamon

1/2 teaspoon ground ginger

8 to 10 baby bananas, peeled and roughly chopped

Preheat oven to 375°F. Using a mixer, cream the butter with the brown sugar, honey, and banana puree. Add the eggs one at a time and continue beating until smooth. Scrape the sides of the bowl with a spatula, and beat again until smooth.

In a separate bowl, stir together the flour, almonds, salt, baking soda, cinnamon, and ginger. Fold these dry ingredients into the wet mixture until smooth. Fold in the chopped baby bananas.

Prepare a 10-inch round cake pan (or the ramekins) by brushing with oil or melted butter and dusting with flour, tapping out any excess. Pour the batter into the pan and bake for 30 to 35 minutes (or 25 to 30 minutes for individual cakes), or until a knife inserted into the center comes out clean. Remove from oven and allow to cool 5 to 7 minutes before serving. Slice and serve with Chocolate-Cinnamon Ice Cream or other store-bought ice cream of your choice.

Upside-Down Pineapple Tart

Here's a tropical version of a classic apple tart tatin, with slices of pineapple baked in caramel on the bottom of the pan. It is an excellent dessert for cold weather or holiday meals. Bake the tart in any pan that has 1 1/2- to 2-inch-high sides. Serve with Piñon-Caramel Ice Cream (page 23) or Pineapple Sorbet (page 10).

1 large pineapple

1 cup sugar

2 tablespoons unsalted butter

1/2 teaspoon ground cloves

1 sheet puff pastry

Preheat oven to 400°F. Using a sharp chef's knife, trim the top and bottom off the pineapple and then slice off the skin, working your way around the fruit. Cut in quarters lengthwise from top to bottom. Trim the core from each piece and cut the quarters into 2-inch-thick chunks.

Sprinkle the sugar into a sauté pan and place over medium heat. Allow the sugar to melt and brown. When it is dark amber colored, caramelized, and lightly smoking, carefully add the butter, pineapple chunks, and ground cloves. Cook the pineapple in the caramel for 3 to 4 minutes, turning the chunks from side to side, so they can soak up the caramel and release their juices. Remove from heat.

Prepare a 10-inch cake pan with 1 1/2- to 2-inch-high sides by brushing with oil or melted butter. Pour the pineapple-caramel mixture into the prepared pan. Cut the sheet of puff pastry into a circle slightly larger than the pan, about 10 1/2 inches in diameter. Fit the puff pastry circle into the pan over the pineapple. Bake in the oven for 30 to 35 minutes. Remove from the oven and allow to cool for 15 minutes. While the tart is still warm, place a large plate over the top of the pan and invert. Slowly pull the cake pan off the upside down tart. If you have difficulties, return it to a hot oven for a few minutes to melt and loosen the caramel. It should then be easily removed. You may rewarm the tart this way before serving if you make it ahead of time. After inverting the tart and removing the pan, slice it into wedges and place on individual plates.

Brazil Nut Frangipane Asian Pear Strudel

Fruit strudels, usually made with apples or pears, are a classic European dessert preparation. In this recipe, their familiar form is reinspired and internationalized with the use of New World Brazil nuts and Asian pears from the Far East. Frangipane is a sweet pastry cream traditionally flavored with almonds, and was named after a 16th-century Italian nobleman, Marquis Muzio Frangipani, who invented a bitter almond perfume. I hope Marquis Frangipani takes no offense at my Brazil nut interpretation of the pastry cream bearing his name—perhaps he would have invented Brazil nut perfume if he had access to tropical rain forest products like we do today! I suggest topping these strudels with Tropical Nut Brittle Ice Cream (page 21) or Coconut Ice Cream (page 18).

1 cup Brazil nuts

1/2 cup (1 stick) unsalted butter, softened

1/2 cup brown sugar

2 eggs

1/4 cup all-purpose flour

1/2 teaspoon ground allspice

2 Asian pears, cored and cut into 1/2- to 1-inch pieces

4 sheets phyllo dough

1/4 cup (1/2 stick) unsalted butter, melted

1/4 cup powdered sugar

Preheat oven to 350°F. Spread the Brazil nuts on a dry cookie sheet and roast in the oven for 14 to 16 minutes, until golden brown. Remove from the nuts from the oven and increase the temperature to 400°F. Place the nuts in a food processor and pulverize for 15 to 20 seconds. Add the softened butter and brown sugar and process for another 30 seconds. Continue pulverizing while adding the eggs one at a time, the flour, and finally the allspice. Transfer the mixture to a bowl and fold in the chunks of Asian pear. Set aside.

Place 2 sheets of phyllo side by side on a work surface. Brush with the melted butter and use a sifter to dust it with powdered sugar. Place the 2 remaining sheets of phyllo on top of these, and press firmly with the palms of your hands to seal each set of two sheets together. Brush the tops with melted butter and dust with sifted powdered sugar. Spoon half of the Brazil nut–Asian pear filling along a longer edge of one set of layered phyllo. Grasp onto the long edge, and carefully roll the filling up into the phyllo, pressing with your fingers to ensure as tight a roll as possible. Repeat with the second set of layered phyllo to create a second strudel. Transfer each strudel to a parchment-lined cookie sheet. If desired, you may refrigerate the strudels at this point for several hours. When ready to serve, bake them at 400°F for 16 to 18 minutes, until golden brown. Remove from oven and allow to cool for a few minutes. Slice into 4-inch-long pieces and serve on warm plates. If desired, top with a scoop of ice cream.

Brazil Nut Frangipane Asian Pear Strudel

Guava Jam Linzer Torte

MAKES ONE *10*-INCH ROUND TART, OR *8* TO *10* SERVINGS

Classic linzer tortes, which originated in Linz, Austria, are made from shortbread crust flavored with lemon, cinnamon, and nuts and filled with blackberry or raspberry preserves. In my tropical interpretation, the crust is flavored with an assortment of tropical nuts and a touch of nutmeg, and the filling is a simple "jam" of reduced, pureed fresh guavas. This dessert is perfect for a light lunch or afternoon tea gathering. For a slightly richer dessert, serve it with Coconut Ice Cream (page 18) or Guava Sorbet (page 12).

For the tropical nut linzer dough

1/2 cup cashews

1/2 cup macadamias

1/2 cup Brazil nuts

3/4 cup powdered sugar

1 cup (2 sticks) unsalted butter

2 eggs

1/2 teaspoon vanilla extract

2 cups all-purpose flour

1/2 teaspoon ground nutmeg

For the guava filling

6 guavas, ripe but still a bit firm (or substitute 6 feijoas)

Juice of 1 lime

1/4 cup sugar

1/4 teaspoon ground cinnamon

To prepare the linzer dough, preheat the oven to 375°F. Spread all the nuts on a dry cookie sheet and roast in the oven for 14 to 16 minutes, until golden brown. Remove them from the oven, turn off the oven, and allow the nuts to cool for a few minutes. Place the nuts in a food processor and pulverize for 20 seconds. Add the powdered sugar and butter and continue to process. Add the eggs one at a time, then the vanilla extract, and process until smooth. In a separate bowl, stir together the flour and nutmeg. Add these dry ingredients to the food processor and pulse several times. Turn the mixture out into a bowl and work it together with your hands until combined. Wrap the dough in plastic wrap and refrigerate until well chilled, at least 1/2 hour.

You can make the guava filling while the dough chills. Peel the guavas, roughly chop the fruit, and combine them in a blender with the lime juice. Puree the guavas, pushing them down inside the blender with a wooden spoon, if necessary. Puree for 30 seconds, then pass the puree through a fine strainer into a saucepan. Add the sugar and cinnamon and place over medium-low heat. Simmer the mixture for 20 minutes, stirring periodically, until it is slightly reduced and thickened. Turn off the heat, and place the guava jam in the refrigerator until it is thoroughly cooled.

Preheat oven to 350°F. Prepare a 10-inch tart pan by brushing with oil or melted butter and dusting with flour, tapping out any excess. On a well-floured work surface, roll the linzer dough to 1/8 to 1/4 inch thick. Cut a circle 2 inches larger in diameter than the tart pan and roll it up onto the rolling pin. Roll it out onto the prepared tart pan and use your fingers to press the dough into the corners, flattening out the bottom and evening out the top edge. Using a rubber spatula, transfer the guava jam into the crust and distribute it evenly. Cut the excess dough into twelve to fourteen 1-inch pieces. On the floured work surface, roll the pieces into long snakelike strips approximately 1/8 to 1/4 inch in diameter. Lay half of the strips in parallel fashion approximately 1 inch apart from each other, then lay the remaining strips across the first layer at a 45° angle. Bake the linzer torte for 35 to 40 minutes, until the edges of the crust are lightly browned. Remove from the oven and allow to cool for a few minutes. Slice and serve while still warm.

Caramel and Plantain Tart

MAKES ONE 10-INCH TART, OR 8 TO 10 SERVINGS

During plantain season in West Africa, Donna and I made caramelized plantains every morning to liven up our oatmeal. I knew then that caramel and plantains would make a fabulous dessert! Be sure to use very ripe plantains, with blackened skins and soft flesh. Serve this tasty tart with Tropical Nut Brittle Ice Cream (page 21) or Double Vanilla Ice Cream (page 21), or Roasted Banana Sorbet (page 17).

For the crust

1/2 cup (1 stick) unsalted butter

1 1/4 cups all-purpose flour

1 teaspoon ground ginger

1/2 teaspoon salt

2 teaspoons sugar

1/4 cup cold milk or water

For the filling

1/2 cup sugar

1/4 cup heavy cream

1/4 cup (1/2 stick) unsalted butter, melted

3 eggs

1/2 teaspoon vanilla extract

1/2 teaspoon salt

1/2 teaspoon ground cinnamon

2 plantains, ripened until black and sliced diagonally into 1/8-inch-thick slices

To prepare the crust, cut the butter into 1/2-inch pieces and combine in a mixing bowl with the flour, ginger, salt, and sugar. Using the paddle attachment, mix on low speed until the butter is broken into bits and the mixture is crumbly. Add the cold milk or water and pulse the mixer a few times. Turn the dough out onto a work surface and work it together with your hands. Wrap in plastic wrap and chill in the refrigerator for at least 20 minutes.

Preheat oven to 375°F. On a well-floured work surface, roll the dough to 1/8 inch thick. Dust with flour as necessary to keep the dough manageable and prevent it from sticking. Prepare an 8- or 10-inch tart pan by greasing with butter or oil and dusting with flour, tapping out any excess. Transfer the dough to the pan by rolling it onto the rolling pin, then out into the pan. Carefully press the dough into the bottom of the pan and around the sides. You can cut off excess overhanging dough by rolling the pin over the top of the shell. Place a large piece of aluminum foil inside the tart shell and fill with pie weights or other dry weights, such as dried beans or rice. This will prevent the dough from bubbling as it "blind bakes." Bake for 12 to 14 minutes. Remove the foil and weights and brush the inside of the tart shell with egg white in order to seal it. Return to the oven and bake for another 3 minutes. Remove and allow to cool. Reduce the oven temperature to 325°F.

For the filling, sprinkle the sugar into a sauté pan and place over medium heat. Allow the sugar to melt and caramelize. When it darkens and begins to lightly smoke, carefully add the cream, and stir to dissolve any lumps of caramel. Cool the caramel by transferring it to a large bowl and placing in the refrigerator. Whisk the melted butter and eggs into the cooled caramel. Add the vanilla, salt, and cinnamon and whisk well. Fold the plantain slices into the mixture.

Pour the filling into the baked tart shell. Bake for 45 to 50 minutes, until the filling is well set and doesn't ripple when you tap the side of the tart pan. Remove from oven and allow to cool. Cut the tart into wedges and serve while still warm.

> *Among thornless lote-trees*
> *And clustered plantains,*
> *And spreading shade,*
> *And water gushing,*
> *And fruit in plenty*
> *Neither out of reach nor yet forbidden.*
> —SURAH LVI, *KORAN*

Warm Persimmon Tart

MAKES ONE 10-INCH TART, OR **8** TO **10** SERVINGS

Persimmons, or kaki, are a favorite Japanese fruit, and images of them abound in Japanese poetry and literature. The key to successfully making this recipe is using very ripe persimmons, as unripe ones will be unpleasantly tart and tannic. Choose fruits that are deep orange in color and jamlike soft to the touch. I suggest topping this delicious warm tart with a scoop of Kumquat-Orange Sorbet (page 13), Kiwi Sorbet (page 12), or Sesame Brittle Ice Cream (page 19).

4 persimmons, preferably the Hachiyin variety, ripe and very soft

1 cup plain yogurt

2 tablespoons honey

2 tablespoons brown sugar

1/2 teaspoon ground cardamom

1/2 teaspoon ground cinnamon

1 sheet puff pastry

1 tablespoon sugar

Using a sharp paring knife, cut the leaf stem from the persimmon. Cut through the skin, scoring the fruit lengthwise from one end to the other in 4 to 6 places. Peel the skin off the fruit, using the paring knife, if necessary. Cut the soft fruits into quarters and set aside.

In a bowl, whisk together the yogurt, honey, brown sugar, cardamom, and cinnamon. Set aside.

Preheat oven to 400°F. Cut a 10-inch circle from the puff pastry sheet and place it on a parchment-lined cookie sheet. Bake for 16 to 18 minutes until the pastry is puffed up and browned. Remove from oven and allow to cool. Heat the broiler.

With a sharp paring knife, cut a circle in the top of the puff pastry round 1/2 inch smaller than the outside diameter of the pastry. Gently press the center down, to create a pielike form with a depressed center and higher rim around the edges. Using a rubber spatula, transfer the yogurt mixture into the puffed pastry and distribute it evenly. Arrange the persimmons over the yogurt and sprinkle with the tablespoon of sugar. Place under a preheated broiler for approximately 30 seconds, just long enough to melt the sugar, watching it closely and turning as necessary. Slice into pieces and serve warm with a fruit sorbet or vanilla ice cream.

Pecan-Molasses Pie

MAKES ONE 8- TO 10-INCH PIE, OR 8 TO 10 SERVINGS

Here's my version of a classic Southern pecan pie, sweetened with thick, rich molasses. Molasses is the syrup separated from raw sugar cane during the refinement process. Use any kind of good-quality molasses for this recipe, but not the dark "blackstrap" molasses, which is the poorest grade. For a more decadent dessert, top slices of this pie with Chocolate-Cinnamon Ice Cream (page 18), Molasses Ice Cream (page 20), or Roasted Banana Sorbet (page 17).

For the crust

1/2 **cup (1 stick) unsalted butter**

3/4 **cup all-purpose flour**

2 **tablespoons sugar**

1 **egg**

1 **tablespoon cold water**

For the filling

3 **eggs**

1 **cup molasses**

1/4 **cup (1/2 stick) unsalted butter, melted**

1/2 **cup sugar**

1 **tablespoon all-purpose flour**

1/2 **teaspoon salt**

1/2 **teaspoon vanilla extract**

1/2 **teaspoon ground star anise**

1 1/2 **cups pecans**

To make the crust, cut the butter into 1/2-inch pieces and combine in a mixing bowl with the flour and sugar. Using the paddle attachment, mix on low speed until the butter is broken into bits and the mixture is crumbly. Add the egg and cold water and continue to mix for another minute, until the dough comes together. Wrap in plastic wrap and chill in the refrigerator for at least 20 minutes.

Preheat oven to 375°F. On a well-floured work surface, roll the dough to 1/8 inch thick. Dust with flour as necessary to keep the dough manageable and prevent it from sticking. Prepare an 8- or 10-inch pie pan or tart pan by greasing with butter or oil and dusting with flour, tapping out any excess. Transfer the dough to the pan by rolling it onto the rolling pin, then out into the pan. Carefully press the dough into the bottom of the pan and around the sides. You can cut off excess overhanging dough by rolling the pin over the top of the shell. Place a large piece of aluminum foil inside the tart shell and fill with pie weights or other dry weights, such as dried beans or rice. This will prevent the dough from bubbling as it "blind bakes." Bake for 12 to 14 minutes. Remove the foil and weights and brush the inside of the tart shell with egg white in order to seal it. Return to the oven and bake for another 3 minutes. Remove and allow to cool. Reduce the oven temperature to 325°F.

For the filling, in a large bowl, whisk together the eggs, molasses, melted butter, and sugar until smooth. Whisk in all remaining ingredients. Pour into the prebaked pie shell and bake in the oven for 55 to 60 minutes. When finished, the center of the filling should be well set when the edge of the pan is tapped. Remove from oven and allow to cool for 10 minutes before cutting and serving.

Green Mango–Green Apple Pie

*MAKES ONE 10-INCH PIE, OR **8** TO **10** SERVINGS*

Although an unlikely combination, green mangoes make a tasty tropical partner for Granny Smith apples. Apples are a favorite American and European fruit, but mangoes are better known around the world than apples. They're a staple tropical fruit, second only to bananas and coconuts in widespread cultivation. Some estimates claim mangoes have been cultivated for as long as six thousand years. Both green mangoes and green apples are excellent for baking because of their tartness. Serve this unique apple pie à la mode with sweet Passion Fruit Sorbet (page 10) or Double Vanilla Ice Cream (page 21).

For the crust

1 cup (2 sticks) unsalted butter

1 1/2 cups all-purpose flour

1 teaspoon salt

2 teaspoons sugar

1/2 cup cold water

For the filling

1 mango, green and just beginning to ripen

2 Granny Smith apples

2 tablespoons brown sugar

1 teaspoon cornstarch

Juice of 1 lemon

1 teaspoon vanilla extract

2 teaspoons rum (optional)

1 teaspoon grated gingerroot

1/2 teaspoon ground cinnamon

1/2 teaspoon ground allspice

1 egg, lightly beaten, for wash

To prepare the crust, cut the butter into 1/2-inch pieces and combine in a mixing bowl with the flour, salt, and sugar. Using the paddle attachment, mix on low speed until the butter is broken into bits and the mixture is crumbly. Add the cold water and pulse the mixer a few times. Turn the dough out onto a work surface and work it together with your hands. Wrap in plastic wrap and chill in the refrigerator for at least 20 minutes.

Preheat oven to 375°F. On a well-floured work surface, roll the dough to 1/8 inch thick. Dust with flour as necessary to keep the dough manageable and prevent it from sticking. Prepare a 10-inch pie pan by greasing with butter or oil and dusting with flour, tapping out any excess. Cut two 12-inch circles from the 1/8-inch-thick dough. You may have to cut one circle, then press the scraps together and roll out the dough a second time for the second circle. Transfer one circle of dough to the pan by rolling it onto the rolling pin, then out into the pan. Carefully press it into the bottom of the pan and around the sides. Set aside.

For the filling, peel the mango, slice the flesh from the large pit, and cut into 1-inch triangular pieces. Peel and core the apples, and cut the fruit into 1-inch chunks. Combine the mango, apple, and all remaining ingredients except the egg in a large bowl, and stir together so they are well mixed.

Pour the filling into the pie crust and mound it slightly in the middle. Use a pastry brush to coat the rim of the lower pie crust with beaten egg. Roll the second circle of dough onto the rolling pin, and then out on top of the pie filling. Using your fingers, press the edges of the lower and upper crust together around the rim of the pan. Trim any overhanging dough from the edges with a sharp paring knife, and pinch a decorative pattern around the rim. Brush the entire top crust with beaten egg and poke a hole in the center of the pie with a paring knife. Bake for 50 to 55 minutes. Cool for 15 minutes before cutting and serving warm on individual plates.

Green Mango–Green Apple Pie with Double Vanilla Ice Cream

Whole Baked Asian Pear with Cashews and Ginger Sabayon

*MAKES **6** SERVINGS*

This dessert was inspired by memories of peeking into the oven as a child, usually after a holiday meal of roasted venison, to impatiently watch hand-picked Vermont apples bake and shrivel in a simple spice topping of brown sugar and cinnamon. In this Far Eastern version, delicious Asian pears filled with roasted cashews intensify in flavor as they bake in a honey coating. To ensure best results, make the ginger sabayon at the last minute before serving. Because of its light Asian character, this dessert would make an excellent ending to a seafood meal.

For the baked Asian pears

1 cup cashews, lightly chopped

1 cup golden raisins

1 cup honey

1 teaspoon ground cinnamon

1/4 teaspoon finely ground black pepper

6 Asian pears

For the sabayon sauce

2 eggs

1 egg yolk

1/2 cup sugar

1/4 cup rum, or brandy or bourbon

2 tablespoons finely grated gingerroot

To prepare the baked pears, preheat oven to 375°F. Spread the cashews on a dry cookie sheet and roast in the oven for 12 to 14 minutes, until golden brown. Remove the nuts from the oven and set aside to cool, leaving the oven temperature at 375°F. Combine the cooled nuts in a bowl with the raisins.

Pour the honey in a saucepan and place over medium heat. When the honey is hot, add the cinnamon and black pepper and stir for 1 1/2 minutes. Place the whole cored pears in a large bowl and pour the hot honey over them. Turn the fruits with a spoon to coat them well with the honey mixture. Place the pears, with cored hole facing up, in a casserole dish and pour the excess honey from the bowl over the pears. Fill the cored holes of the pears with the roasted cashews and raisins. Bake the pears for 45 to 50 minutes, until they are tender.

To make the ginger sabayon, whisk together the eggs, egg yolk, sugar, rum, and ginger in a bowl or double boiler over very hot, but not boiling, water. Whisk continuously and vigorously for 16 to 18 minutes, letting no part of the mixture lay still, until it is light and fluffy. Place the baked Asian pears on individual plates, and spoon some ginger sabayon sauce over the top. Serve immediately.

Whole Baked Asian Pear with Cashews and Ginger Sabayon

Citrus-Papaya Crisp with Honey and Coconut

MAKES ONE 10-INCH SQUARE PAN, OR 12 SERVINGS

Fruit crisps are some of the first desserts I can remember enjoying as a child. My older sister, Lynn, used to bake an apple crisp every week at our Vermont farmhouse, and I'll never forget the delicious, warm flavor of her rolled oat and cinnamon topping. This crisp has a tropical twist, made with citrus and papaya instead of apples, and with fresh coconut shavings added to the cinnamon-oat topping. Enjoy it with Cactus Pear Sorbet (page 12), Coconut Ice Cream (page 18), or Chinese Five-Spice Ice Cream (page 20).

For the filling

1 orange

1 grapefruit

1 lime

1 papaya

1 cup honey

2 teaspoons cornstarch

1/2 teaspoon ground allspice

1/4 teaspoon ground clove

1/2 teaspoon ground star anise

For the topping

1/2 cup (1 stick) unsalted butter, diced into 1/2-inch cubes

1 cup brown sugar

3/4 cup all-purpose flour

1/2 cup rolled oats

1/2 teaspoon ground cinnamon

1 coconut

To prepare the filling, using a sharp chef's knife, trim the tops and bottoms off the orange, grapefruit, and lime, then cut all the peel and pith from the inner flesh, working your way around the fruit. Section the fruits by cutting between each membrane and removing each wedge of fruit. Work over a large bowl in order to catch all the juice, and allow the sections to drop into the bowl. When all the sections are removed, squeeze the membranes to extract as much remaining juice as possible. Peel and halve the papaya, and scrape out the black seeds with a spoon. Cut the papaya flesh into 1-inch chunks and combine them in the bowl with the citrus. Stir the honey into the fruit mixture. In a separate small bowl, stir together the cornstarch and spices. Sprinkle the spice mixture over the fruit and stir thoroughly. Set aside and preheat the oven to 375°F.

To make the topping, in a mixing bowl, combine the butter, brown sugar, flour, oats, and cinnamon. Mix on low speed for 1 1/2 minutes until crumbly. Poke a hole in the "eye" of the coconut and drain the coconut milk into a bowl for another use. Roast the whole coconut in the oven for 20 minutes. Remove and allow to cool. Crack the cooled coconut on a hard surface and pry the flesh from the shell with a large spoon. Use a peeler to make 1 cup of coconut shavings from the white flesh.

Prepare a 10×10×2-inch pan or casserole dish by brushing with oil or melted butter. Pour in the spiced fruit mixture and spread it evenly in the pan. Sprinkle the crumb topping over the fruit, and then sprinkle the coconut shavings over the crumb topping. Bake for 40 to 45 minutes. Allow to cool slightly, and serve while still warm.

Mango Ginger Macadamia Crisp

MAKES ONE 10-INCH SQUARE PAN, OR 12 SERVINGS

In this aromatic crisp, the sweet mangoes are balanced by the spicy bite of fresh minced ginger, while the crunchy clove-spiced topping of macadamia nuts provides a rich counterpart to the luscious, warm fruit. I don't think a warm crisp is ever complete unless it's à la mode—try the Sesame Brittle Ice Cream (page 19) or Passion Fruit Sorbet (page 10).

For the filling

2 mangoes

1/4 cup dark rum

1/2 cup brown sugar

1/2 cup minced gingerroot

Juice of 1 lemon

1/2 teaspoon ground star anise

For the topping

1/2 cup (1 stick) unsalted butter, diced into 1/2-inch cubes

1/2 cup brown sugar

1/2 cup all-purpose flour

1/4 teaspoon ground cloves

3/4 cup macadamia nuts

To prepare the filling, peel the mangoes and slice the flesh from the large, inner pit. Cut the fruit into 1-inch chunks and place them in a bowl. Set aside. Combine the rum, brown sugar, and minced ginger in a saucepan and place over medium heat. Stir as the sugar dissolves and the mixture comes to a simmer. Reduce heat to low and simmer for 6 to 8 minutes, until the ginger becomes slightly translucent. Add the mixture to the mangoes along with the lemon juice and star anise. Stir until well combined. Set aside and preheat oven to 375°F.

To make the topping, in a mixing bowl, combine the butter, brown sugar, flour, and ground cloves. Mix on low speed for 1 1/2 minutes until crumbly. Spread the macadamia nuts on a cutting board or work surface, and press down on them with the side of a chef's knife to lightly crush them. Set the crushed nuts aside.

Prepare a 10×10×2-inch pan or casserole dish by brushing with oil or melted butter. Pour in the mango mixture and spread it evenly in the pan. Sprinkle the crumb topping over the fruit, and then sprinkle the crushed macadamias over the crumb topping. Bake for 40 to 45 minutes. Allow to cool slightly, and serve while still warm.

In all those islands ginger is found, which we ate green like bread. This ginger is not a tree but a small plant which produces and throws out above the ground certain shoots or pipes, a palm in length, like those of reeds, and with the same leaves but narrower and shorter. And these shoots or pipes are worthless, but the root is the ginger, which is not so strong green as when it is dried. And those people dry it in large jars, for otherwise it would not keep.

—ANTONIO PIGAFETTA, *MAGELLAN'S VOYAGE*

Banana Rum Caramel Chocolate Buckle

*MAKES ONE 10-INCH PAN, OR 12 SERVINGS, OR **8** TO **10** INDIVIDUAL DESSERTS*

Buckles are a classic American home-style dessert, named for the pastry topping baked over fruit that takes on a crumpled, buckled texture. Everyone's favorite tropical flavors are included in this version, a decadent combination of bananas soaked in rum and caramel and topped with a rich chocolate buckle topping studded with tropical nuts of your choice. Paradise found! Top it with scoops of Chocolate-Cinnamon Ice Cream (page 18) or Tropical Nut Brittle Ice Cream (page 21).

For the banana filling

7 to 8 bananas

1/2 cup dark rum

1/2 teaspoon ground allspice

For the caramel

1 cup sugar

1/4 cup water

For the chocolate buckle topping

1/2 cup (1 stick) unsalted butter, diced into 1/2-inch cubes

6 ounces bittersweet chocolate, melted

1/4 cup sugar

1 1/4 cups all-purpose flour

1/4 cup cocoa powder

1/2 cup tropical nuts of your choice, such as cashews, macadamias, or peanuts (optional)

To prepare the filling, peel the bananas and cut in half crosswise, then cut each half lengthwise into quarters to create approximate 3-inch strips. Toss the banana strips in a bowl with the rum and allspice. Divide the banana mixture among 8 to 10 individual ungreased 4-ounce ramekins, or place them in a 10-inch ungreased casserole dish or pie pan. Set aside.

To make the caramel, sprinkle the sugar in a sauté pan and place over medium heat. Allow the sugar to melt and begin to caramelize. When it is browned and lightly smoking, carefully add the water while stirring. Reduce heat to low and continue stirring until the caramel is completely dissolved. Pour the caramel over the bananas in the ramekins or pie dish.

For the topping, preheat the oven to 375°F. Combine the butter and chocolate in a mixing bowl and mix on low speed. Add the sugar, flour, and cocoa powder and mix for 1 minute, until the mixture pulls together into a crumbly mass. Lightly pack the topping over the bananas, dividing it among the ramekins or using the entire mixture in the pie dish. Sprinkle the nuts over the top, and bake for 40 to 45 minutes. Allow to cool slightly, and serve while still warm.

Banana Rum Caramel Chocolate Buckle

Cinnamon Buñuelos with Bananas and Chocolate Sauce

MAKES **6** TO **8** SERVINGS

Buñuelos are Latin American pastries that are deep-fried and sprinkled with powdered sugar. This dessert, one of our most popular at the Coyote Cafe, combines the classic Mexican flavors of cinnamon, chocolate, and banana. Cinnamon-flavored buñuelos are served with fresh bananas sautéed in brown sugar and dark beer, drizzled with a simple chocolate sauce. Muy rica! If desired, serve with Roasted Banana Sorbet (page 17) or Double Vanilla Ice Cream (page 21).

For the buñuelos

1 cup all-purpose flour

1/2 cup (1 stick) unsalted butter, cold and diced into 1/2-inch cubes

1/2 teaspoon salt

1 teaspoon sugar

1/4 teaspoon baking powder

2 teaspoons ground cinnamon

1/4 cup water

3 cups oil for frying, such as peanut or canola

Powdered sugar for dusting

For the chocolate sauce

6 ounces (about 1 1/2 cups chopped) bittersweet chocolate, melted

1/2 cup hot water

For the bananas

4 bananas

1/4 cup brown sugar

1/4 cup dark beer, such as stout or porter

To make the buñuelos, combine the flour, butter, salt, sugar, baking powder, and cinnamon in a mixing bowl and mix on low speed until the butter is completely broken up into small bits in the dry ingredients, about 4 to 5 minutes. Pour in the water and mix on medium speed for 8 to 10 minutes. As the dough comes together in clumps, continue mixing into a firm dough. Wrap it in plastic wrap and refrigerate for 20 minutes. On a well-floured work surface, roll the chilled dough out very thin, approximately 1/16 inch. Sprinkle with flour as necessary while working with it to prevent sticking. Cut out 6 to 8 triangles that are 5 inches long on each edge.

Place the frying oil in a large saucepan over medium heat. Allow it to heat for 4 to 5 minutes until it reaches frying temperature of 325° to 350°F, then reduce the heat to low. You can test the oil temperature by dropping a small scrap of dough into it. The dough should rapidly sizzle and rise to the top. When the oil is ready, carefully drop a few triangles of dough in and allow them to deep fry for 1 1/2 minutes on each side, or until their sizzling subsides, turning them with a slotted spoon. Drain the fried buñuelos on a cookie sheet lined with paper towels.

To continue with the recipe, whisk together the melted chocolate and hot water until smooth. Set aside until ready to serve. Peel the bananas and cut them in half crosswise, then cut each half lengthwise into quarters. Combine the brown sugar and beer in a sauté pan and place over medium heat. Allow the sugar to dissolve and the mixture to begin to boil, then add the banana strips and sauté, tossing or stirring the bananas, for 3 to 4 minutes. Divide the hot bananas in piles in the centers of 6 to 8 plates. Dust the buñuelos with powdered sugar and place one on top of each pile of bananas. Drizzle chocolate sauce around the dessert and serve immediately.

Dark Rum Bread Pudding with Ginger and Papaya

MAKES ONE *10-INCH SQUARE PAN*, OR *12* SERVINGS

Bread puddings are beloved desserts around the world, and a great way to use up that stale loaf of French bread leftover from dinner the other night! I've nicknamed this dessert "Island Pudding" because of its use of dark rum—preferably a Jamaican variety—fresh papaya, and ginger. The spicy custard is also flavored with a hint of nutmeg, a touch of cocoa powder, and a pinch of black pepper to give it complexity. If you'd like to serve it with an ice cream, I suggest Coconut (page 18) or Tropical Nut Brittle (page 21).

1/4 cup macadamia nuts (optional)

3 eggs

1/2 cup sugar

2 tablespoons honey

1/2 cup milk

1/2 cup heavy cream

6 tablespoons dark rum

1/4 teaspoon ground nutmeg

1/4 teaspoon finely ground black pepper

1 teaspoon cocoa powder

6 cups bread, such as brioche or French, cut into
    1-inch cubes

2 tablespoons minced gingerroot

1 papaya

Preheat oven to 350°F. Spread the nuts on a dry cookie sheet and roast them in the oven for 14 to 16 minutes, until golden brown. Remove them from the oven and turn them out onto a work surface or cutting board. Crush them lightly by pressing down on them with the side of a chef's knife.

In a large bowl, whisk together the eggs, sugar, honey, milk, cream, rum, spices, and cocoa powder. Whisk in the nuts. Add the bread cubes, and push them down into the custard so they can soak it up. Place the bowl in the refrigerator for 1/2 hour. Remove from the refrigerator and stir in the minced ginger. Peel the papaya, slice it in half, and scrape the seeds out with a spoon. Cut the papaya into 1/2- to 1-inch chunks and stir them into the bread-custard mixture.

Prepare a 10×10×2-inch pan by brushing it with melted butter or oil. Pour in the bread pudding mixture and bake for 50 to 55 minutes. Check the pudding halfway through the baking time, and if it is browning too much on top cover it with foil. Remove the pudding from the oven when done, and allow it to cool for 10 minutes before serving.

Jasmine Rice Pudding with Honey, Tamarind, and Almonds

MAKES ONE 10-INCH SQUARE PAN, OR 12 SERVINGS

Jasmine rice is a long-grained white Asian variety with a distinctive, perfumed taste that makes a delicious and delicate rice pudding, enjoyed as traditional and satisfying home-style desserts in many regions around the world. In this recipe, tangy tamarind gives every bite an unexpected burst of flavor, topped with a rich caramelized honey sauce and roasted almonds. If you can't readily find jasmine rice, regular long-grain rice can be substituted.

For the rice pudding

3 cups milk

3/4 cup tamarind pulp (3 or 4 pods)

1 cup jasmine rice

2/3 cup sugar

1/2 teaspoon vanilla extract

Pinch of salt

2 tablespoons unsalted butter

4 eggs, separated

For the roasted almonds

1/2 cup almonds, sliced

For the honey sauce

1/2 cup honey

1/4 cup water

To prepare the pudding, combine the milk and tamarind pulp in a saucepan and place over medium heat. Bring the milk to a simmer to soften the tamarind, then remove from heat. Pass the mixture through a fine strainer into a bowl, pressing tender tamarind pulp through the strainer with your fingers to separate it from any seeds or bits of tough pulp. Return the mixture to the saucepan and add the rice, sugar, vanilla, salt, and butter. Place over medium heat and bring to a boil. Reduce the heat to low and simmer the rice for 20 minutes.

Preheat oven to 375°F. Remove the rice from the heat and allow to cool 10 minutes. Whisk in the egg yolks until well combined. Using a mixer, whip the egg whites to stiff peaks. Fold them into the rice custard. Prepare a 10×10×2-inch casserole dish by brushing it with oil or melted butter. Transfer the pudding mixture to the dish, and place it in any kind of larger pan that is filled with 1/2 inch of water. This "water bath" will allow the rice pudding to cook gently. Bake for 40 to 45 minutes. Remove from the oven and allow to cool. Leave the oven temperature at 375°F.

To roast the almonds, spread the sliced almonds on a dry cookie sheet and roast them in the oven for 12 to 14 minutes, until golden brown. Remove from the oven and set aside until ready to serve.

You can make the honey sauce while the pudding is baking. Place the honey in a saucepan over medium-high heat and bring it to a boil, so that it begins to brown and lightly smoke. When it is caramelizing and lightly smoking, carefully add the water, stirring with a whisk to dissolve any clumps of honey. Remove from heat and set aside. Cut the rice pudding in portions and transfer them to plates with a spatula. Drizzle the honey sauce over the pudding and sprinkle with the fresh roasted almonds. Serve immediately.

Tapioca Spiced Pudding with Papaya and Banana

Tapioca is a starchy extract from the manioc or cassava plant, a root that is widely cultivated in Africa, South America, and Central America. When we lived in West Africa, fresh tapioca pudding could be purchased from sellers in the markets, especially during the manioc harvest season. This pudding was inspired by images of fields filled with manioc plants, with their bright green leaves fluttering in the savanna breeze, ringed by papaya trees laden with magnificent, large green fruits. Serve the pudding in glasses or dessert goblets, accompanied by Aniseed Cookies (page 138) or Pineapple Sorbet (page 10).

2 cups milk

1/4 cup sugar

1/2 teaspoon vanilla extract

1/2 cup tapioca pearls

2 eggs, separated

1/2 cup powdered sugar

1/4 teaspoon ground allspice

1/4 teaspoon ground ginger

1/4 teaspoon ground aniseed

1 banana

1 papaya

Preheat oven to 375°F. Combine the milk, sugar, and vanilla extract in a saucepan and place over medium heat. When it comes to a boil, sprinkle in the tapioca pearls and stir well. Remove from the heat, and whisk in the egg yolks. Using a mixer, whip the egg whites with the powdered sugar to stiff peaks. Fold the whipped whites and spices into the tapioca mixture. Peel the banana and roughly chop it into 1/2- to 1-inch pieces. Peel the papaya, slice it in half, and remove the black seeds with a spoon. Cut the fruit into 1/2- to 1-inch pieces. Stir the banana and papaya pieces into the tapioca mixture.

Prepare a 10×10×2-inch casserole dish by brushing it with oil or melted butter. Transfer the pudding mixture to the dish and bake at 375°F for 40 to 45 minutes. Remove from oven and allow to cool 10 minutes before serving.

"Island" Morning Mango French Toast

MAKES *6* TO *8* SERVINGS

In France, pain perdu ("lost bread")—what we call French toast—was originally served as a dessert, especially on Easter feast days. This versatile recipe would be equally delicious for breakfast, brunch, or dessert. This rich and fruity, tropics-inspired version is spiced with vanilla and allspice and topped with a simple mango "syrup." The rich whipped cream is flavored with cinnamon and rum, a decadent topping to finish off a delicious dish!

For the toast

1 loaf French bread or brioche

1 mango

1 1/2 cups milk

1/2 teaspoon vanilla extract

1/2 teaspoon ground allspice

1/4 cup honey

1 egg

For the mango syrup

1 mango

1/2 cup honey

1 cup orange juice

For the whipped cream

1/2 cup heavy cream

2 tablespoons sugar

2 tablespoons dark rum

1 teaspoon ground cinnamon

To prepare the toast, slice the bread into approximately eighteen 1/2-inch-thick slices and set aside. Peel the mango, cut the flesh from the large pit, and roughly chop it into large pieces. Combine the milk, vanilla extract, and roughly chopped mango in a blender and puree until smooth, about 30 seconds. Add the allspice, honey, and egg and blend for another 30 seconds. Pour the mixture into a large bowl. Place the bread slices into it, plunging and turning them with a fork so they soak up the mixture. Cover and place in the refrigerator.

To make the mango syrup, peel the mango and cut the flesh from the large pit. Slice half of the flesh very thinly and set aside. Roughly chop the remaining fruit and combine it in the blender with the honey and orange juice. Puree for 30 seconds, or until smooth. Set aside until ready to serve.

Whip the cream to stiff peaks with the sugar, rum, and cinnamon. Set aside until ready to serve.

To cook the toast, heat 2 teaspoons vegetable oil or melt a small amount of butter in a large nonstick sauté pan over medium heat. Place as many slices of toast in the pan as will fit, and reduce the heat to medium-low. Cook until the toast is golden brown in color, then turn and brown the other side. Remove the toast and place on a plate in a warm oven until all the slices have been cooked. Stacks of 2 to 3 slices of toast on plates with the reserved fresh mango layered between them. Drizzle with the mango syrup and top with a dollop of whipped cream.

Pineapple Pancakes with Vanilla Sauce

MAKES *12* TO *14* FOUR-INCH PANCAKES, OR *6* TO *7* SERVINGS

Surprise family and guests on a special Sunday morning with these delicious and unique pancakes, or serve them in smaller quantities as an unexpected dessert. Fruit-studded pancakes were a tradition in my family when I was young, although we usually used Vermont apples or berries. Chunks of luscious sweet pineapple and hints of cinnamon and ginger liven up these pancakes, which are topped with a rich vanilla sauce instead of maple syrup.

For the vanilla sauce

1 cup milk

1/2 vanilla bean, split and scraped

2 egg yolks

2 tablespoons honey

For the pancakes

2/3 cup all-purpose flour

1 tablespoon brown sugar

1 teaspoon baking powder

1/2 teaspoon baking soda

1/2 teaspoon ground cinnamon

1/2 teaspoon ground ginger

3/4 cup milk

1 egg

1 tablespoon butter, melted

1 pineapple, peeled, cored, and cut into 1/2-inch chunks

Vegetable oil or butter for frying

To prepare the vanilla sauce, combine the milk and vanilla bean in a saucepan, place over medium-high heat, and bring to a boil. In a separate bowl, whisk together the yolks and honey. Pour the boiling milk into the yolks while stirring. Return the mixture to the saucepan and cook over medium heat, stirring constantly, until it thickens and coats the back of a spoon. Do not allow the mixture to boil. Pass the sauce through a fine strainer and refrigerate until ready to serve.

To make the pancakes, in a medium bowl, stir together the flour, brown sugar, baking powder, baking soda, and spices. Set aside. In a separate bowl, whisk together the milk, egg, melted butter, and all but 1/2 cup of the pineapple. Stir the dry mixture into the wet mixture until just combined. Heat 2 teaspoons vegetable oil or melt a small amount of butter in a large nonstick sauté pan over medium heat, allowing it to get very hot but not to smoking point. Spoon batter into the hot pan to form 2 to 3 pancakes and cook until the bottoms are golden brown. Flip once and brown the other side. You can place the pancakes on a plate in a warm oven until they have all been cooked. Serve them warm topped with some remaining fresh pineapple and drizzled with vanilla sauce.

Cuban Grilled Bananas with Cinnamon Crêpes and Rum Syrup

MAKES **6** SERVINGS

This dessert is perfect for an outdoor summer barbecue—drop these cinnamon spiced bananas on the grill before the coals die down for a real fire-roasted fresh treat reminiscent of south-of-the-border and island cooking. The bananas are served with cinnamon crêpes and topped with a rich brown sugar–rum sauce. Serve with Chocolate-Cinnamon Ice Cream (page 18), Roasted Banana Sorbet (page 17) or Double Vanilla Ice Cream (page 21).

For the crêpes

1/2 **cup milk**

1/2 **cup all-purpose flour**

1 **teaspoon ground cinnamon**

1 **egg**

2 **teaspoons butter, melted**

For the rum syrup

1/4 **cup water**

1/4 **cup dark rum**

1 **tablespoon corn syrup, preferably dark**

1 **tablespoon brown sugar**

For the grilled bananas

3 **bananas**

1/4 **cup sugar**

1 **teaspoon ground cinnamon**

To make the crêpes, in a bowl, whisk together the milk, flour, cinnamon, egg, and melted butter until smooth. Lightly coat a crêpe pan or small sauté pan with oil, or use a nonstick pan, and place over medium–high heat for 30 seconds. Spoon approximately 2 tablespoons of the crêpe batter into the center of the pan, and quickly tilt the pan from side to side to thinly spread the batter over the bottom. Cook the crêpe for about 20 seconds on each side, turning it gently with a spatula or flipping it in the air. Slide the cooked crêpe onto a plate and continue until to use all the batter, making 6 to 8 crêpes.

Combine all the syrup ingredients in a saucepan, place over medium heat, and bring to a boil. Allow to boil for 3 to 4 minutes. Remove from the heat and set aside.

To grill the bananas, peel the bananas and slice them in half, lengthwise, so that the cut side is flat and not curved. Stir together the sugar and cinnamon in a bowl. Press the banana halves into the cinnamon sugar to coat them well. Over an open fire grill or gas grill with good heat, grill the bananas for about 30 seconds one each side, turning them carefully with a spatula. Remove them when they have distinct markings and are slightly softened. Fold each crêpe into quarters and place on individual plates. Top with a grilled banana and drizzle with the rum syrup.

> *Banana day is my special day,*
> *I cut my stems an I'm on m'way,*
> *Load up de donkey, leave the lan*
> *Head down de hill to banana stan,*
> *When de truck comes roun I take a ride*
> *All de way down to de harbour side—*
> *Dat is de night, when you, touris man,*
> *Would change your place wid a banana man.*
> *Yes, by God, an m'big right han*
> *I will live an die a banana man.*
>
> —EVAN JONES, FROM
> "THE SONG OF THE BANANA MAN"

Cajeta Crêpes with Figs and Piñons

MAKES *6* SERVINGS

Cajeta is caramelized goat's milk, widely used in traditional Mexican desserts. If you like goat cheese, you'll love cajeta's tangy rich and rustic caramel flavor. It's a perfect match for sweet, luscious figs and fresh-roasted piñon nuts. I recommend serving this dessert with a scoop of Cardamom Brittle Ice Cream (page 22) or Double Vanilla Ice Cream (page 21). You should be able to find evaporated goat's milk in most supermarkets and specialty food stores.

For the cajeta caramel

4 cups evaporated goat's milk

2 cups milk

4 teaspoons cornstarch

1 cup sugar

1/4 cup water

For the crepes

1/2 cup milk

1/2 cup all-purpose flour

1/2 teaspoon finely ground black pepper

1 egg

2 teaspoons butter, melted

For the roasted piñons

1/2 cup piñons

For the filling

12 figs (preferable Black Mission)

2 tablespoons honey

1 tablespoon red wine

To make the cajeta caramel, combine the goat's milk and milk in a large saucepan and place over medium-high heat. Bring to a boil, then reduce heat to low to allow the mixture to simmer. Place the cornstarch in a small bowl, and add about 1/2 cup of the hot milk to it, stirring until the cornstarch is dissolved. Whisk this back into the simmering milk mixture.

Meanwhile, combine the water and sugar in a separate saucepan and place over high heat. Allow the sugar to melt and caramelize. It will boil and steam at first, then begin to brown around the sides and continue caramelizing until it turns a deep amber. Remove from the heat and allow to cool for 10 minutes. Carefully ladle approximately 1 cup of the simmering milk into the caramelized sugar, and stir to loosen and dissolve the caramel. Stir this mixture into the remaining milk and continue to simmer until it is reduced, thickened, and dark in color, approximately 1 hour.

Meanwhile, make the crêpes. In a bowl, whisk together the milk, flour, black pepper, egg, and melted butter until smooth. Lightly coat a crêpe pan or small sauté pan with oil, or use a nonstick pan, and place over medium-high heat for 30 seconds. Spoon approximately 2 tablespoons of the crêpe batter into the center of the pan, and quickly tilt the pan from side to side to thinly spread the batter over the bottom. Cook the crêpe for about 20 seconds on each side, turning it gently with a spatula or flipping it in the air. Slide the cooked crêpe onto a plate and continue until to use all the batter, making 6 to 8 crêpes.

To roast the piñons, preheat the oven to 350°F. Spread the piñons on a dry cookie sheet and lightly roast in the oven for 12 to 14 minutes, until golden brown. Remove from the oven and allow to cool.

To prepare the filling, remove the stems from the figs and cut the fruits into quarters. Toss them in a bowl with the honey and red wine. Lay the crêpes out on plates and divide the fig filling between them. Carefully roll the crêpes up. Drizzle generously with warm cajeta caramel sauce, top with roasted piñons, and serve.

Tropical Fruit Spring Rolls

*MAKES **6** SERVINGS*

Asian spring rolls earned their name because they were originally served during new year celebrations, also known in China and Vietnam as spring festivals. Although typically filled with seafood, meat, and vegetables, this playful version of spring rolls bursts with tropical fresh fruit, vanilla, and allspice. They make an excellent ending to any kind of Asian meal, accompanied with scoops of Guava Sorbet (page 12) or Kumquat-Orange Sorbet (page 13).

6 round leaves of rice paper

Assortment of tropical fruits, such as mangoes, papayas, kiwis, figs, and bananas

2 tablespoons brown sugar

1 teaspoon vanilla extract

2 tablespoons sake (or substitute white wine)

1/2 teaspoon ground allspice

Soak the leaves of rice paper in cold water. Prepare the fruits by peeling, pitting, and/or removing their seeds, and cutting them into 1/2-inch chunks. Combine the cut fruit in a bowl with the brown sugar, vanilla extract, sake, and allspice and toss until well mixed. Place a round of rice paper on your work surface and spoon some of the fruit slightly off-center in a 1-inch-thick line. Roll the short side of rice paper over the fruit and roll the circle halfway up. Fold the excess rice paper on the sides into the center, then continuing rolling over to the far edge of the circle to form a spring roll. Repeat with each spring roll. Place the spring rolls in a pan, drizzle with a little water, and heat in a 325°F oven for 12 minutes. Cut them in half diagonally, and place them on individual plates, propping one half up against the other. Serve with a tropical sorbet.

Tropical Fruit Spring Rolls

Pastries and Breads

Tropical and subtropical fruits and nuts make delicious pastries and breads. Most of the recipes in this chapter transform familiar types of pastries and breads, including croissants, brownies, and quick breads using unusual fruits and nuts. Because tropical fruits are not typically thought of as baking ingredients, they can add a unique and playful twist to classic recipes. Most tropical nuts, including Brazil nuts and cashews, are underused in standard baking practices, which tend to favor walnuts and almonds.

These recipes are for simple, home-style baked goods. Refined sugar, often produced from cane sugar grown in the Caribbean, Hawaii, South America, and other tropical regions of the world, is a central ingredient to most baked goods. When sugar was first introduced to European cultures around A.D. 1100, it was a luxury commodity affordable only to the elite and royal classes. At that time, it was considered a tropical and exotic "spice" along with other spices used in this chapter, such as pepper, nutmeg, cardamom, ginger, and cinnamon. It was also widely used for medicinal purposes in subtropical regions of the Mediterranean and North Africa. As sugar production grew with European colonial cultivation of cane on slave-labored plantations, baked goods like tea cakes and quick breads moved out of the realm of royalty and into the common kitchen. Now, we don't consider sugar to be a spice but instead a standard baking ingredient.

The recipes in this chapter make wonderful treats for breakfast, tea time, lunch, or picnics. Grab a homemade tropics-inspired croissant, Danish, or muffin to munch on your way to work, or enjoy these baked goods outdoors on warm spring and summer days, as a finish to lunch or a light meal in themselves, complemented by tea, coffee, or juice. The familiar baking aroma of such spices as cinnamon, nutmeg, clove, and allspice also make for cozy indoor mornings during wintertime or seasonal holiday celebrations. The warmth and comfort of these spices as they fill your kitchen with their sweet aromas transport you to the warm, tropical regions from which they originate.

Cashew Croissants

MAKES **8** TO **10** CROISSANTS

For the dough

11/4 cups milk, at room temperature

1 package (21/2 teaspoons) active dry yeast

4 cups all-purpose flour

1/4 cup sugar

11/2 teaspoons salt

3 tablespoons unsalted butter

3/4 cup (11/2 sticks) unsalted butter, softened

For the filling

2 cups raw, unsalted cashews

2 tablespoons honey

1 egg, lightly beaten

To prepare the dough, pour the milk into a mixing bowl, sprinkle in the yeast, and allow to sit for 2 minutes. Add the flour, sugar, salt, and 3 tablespoons butter. Mix with a dough hook attachment for 6 to 7 minutes on medium speed until dough is a single mass and pulling away from the sides of the bowl. Transfer the dough to an oiled bowl. Cover with plastic wrap. Set the dough aside, allowing it to rest and rise.

After 30 minutes of resting and rising, turn the dough onto a floured surface and sprinkle it with a dusting of flour. Roll into an 8-inch square. Roll the corners of the square outward from the center to create a butterfly shape with a raised square of dough in the center. Spread the 3/4 cup butter onto the square. Fold one corner over the butter and sprinkle its top with a few drops of water. Fold the opposite dough corner over the first corner, and again sprinkle with a few drops of water. Fold another corner over the center, sprinkle with water, then fold the final corner over the top. The dough should now be neatly wrapped around the butter.

Dust the work surface and the dough lightly with flour. Roll the square into a rectangle 15 to 18 inches long. If the butter begins to squeeze extensively out of the dough, transfer to a pan, cover with plastic wrap, and refrigerate for 20 minutes before resuming rolling. When you have a rectangle of the proper size, fold one-third of its length over the middle third, then fold the remaining third over the middle, like folding a letter, to create three equally sized layers. Turn the dough so it lay lengthwise in front of you and roll it into another 15- to 18-inch rectangle. Dust off excess flour and refold into three equally sized layers. Wrap in plastic wrap and rest in the refrigerator for 1 hour. Repeat the above rolling process two more times. Cover the dough with plastic wrap and return it to the refrigerator for an additional hour or overnight.

Preheat the oven to 350°F. Coarsely chop the cashews. Set aside 1/2 cup of the nuts and place the remaining 1 1/2 cups on a cookie sheet and roast in the oven for 14 to 16 minutes, until golden brown. Using a food processor, pulverize the roasted nuts, add the honey, and continue to mix until a thick paste has formed. Set aside. Turn off the oven.

On a floured surface, roll the dough into a rectangle approximately 1/4 to 3/8 inch thick. Cover with plastic wrap and allow to rest for 10 to 15 minutes. Cut the rested dough into pointy triangles approximately 4 to 5 inches on one edge and 6 to 7 inches on the other two edges. Spoon 1 tablespoon of the cashew filling above the short edge of each triangle.

Beginning with the short edge, roll a triangle over the filling and to the point, and tuck the point under the bottom of the rolled croissant. Pull the ends around to make a crescent moon shape. Repeat this process with each triangle, and place each croissant on a parchment-lined cookie sheet, spaced at least 2 1/2 inches apart. Cover the croissants with plastic wrap and place the tray in a warm place (74° to 80°F), such as a stove top above a warm oven. Allow to rise for about 1 hour, or until doubled in size.

Preheat oven to 400°F. Brush the croissants carefully with beaten egg and sprinkle the 1/2 cup of raw cashews over the tops, lightly pressing onto the dough with your fingertips. Bake for 18 to 20 minutes, until the croissants are golden brown.

Cashew Croissants

Macadamia Pain Chocolat

*MAKES **8** TO **10** PASTRIES*

Pain chocolat, *a classic French pastry, is a rectangular-shaped croissant filled with chocolate. It's an enormously popular breakfast pastry, maybe because eating a bit of chocolate in the morning makes us feel decadent and daring! The distinctive and delicate, sweet crunch of macadamia nuts elegantly complements the bittersweet chocolate.*

For the dough

1 cup milk, at room temperature

1 package (2 1/2 teaspoons) active dry yeast

3 3/4 cups all-purpose flour

1 tablespoon cocoa powder

1/4 cup sugar

1 1/2 teaspoons salt

3 tablespoons unsalted butter

3/4 cup (1 1/2 sticks) unsalted butter, softened

For the filling

1 1/2 cups raw, unsalted macadamia nuts

2 tablespoons honey

6 ounces bittersweet chocolate, coarsely chopped

1 egg, lightly beaten

To prepare the dough, see the directions in the previous recipe, Cashew Croissants, p. 107.

Preheat oven to 350°F. Lightly chop or crush all the macadamia nuts, and set aside 1/2 cup. Place the remaining nuts on a cookie sheet and roast in the oven for 14 to 16 minutes. Pulverize the roasted nuts in a food processor, then add the honey and process to a thick paste. Set aside. Turn the oven off.

On a floured surface, roll the dough into a rectangle approximately 1/4 to 3/8 thick. Cover with plastic wrap and allow to rest for 10 to 15 minutes. Cut the dough into 5-inch squares. Spoon one tablespoon of macadamia paste near the bottom edge of each square, and divide the chopped bittersweet chocolate among the squares, placing next to the nut paste. Roll the filling and chocolate up into the dough, until the outer edge is tucked underneath the pastry. Place each pastry on a parchment-lined cookie sheet, at least 2 1/2 inches apart. Cover with plastic wrap and place the tray in a warm place (74° to 80°F), such as a stove top above a warm oven. Allow to rise for 1 hour, or until doubled in size.

Preheat the oven to 400°F. Lightly brush the pastries with beaten egg and sprinkle with the reserved 1/2 cup of crushed raw macadamias. Bake for 18 to 20 minutes or until a deep golden brown. Cool on a rack and serve.

Cardamom-Mango Danish

MAKES **8** TO **10** DANISH

In America, we usually expect our Danishes to be filled with small amounts of fruit or cheese. In Scandinavia, Danishes are called Wienerbröd ("bread from Vienna"), and can refer to any form of rich, delicate bread. The cardamom-spiced mango in this Danish recipe reminds one of an Indian chutney, a highly spiced and sweetened jamlike condiment that is often made with tropical fruits. The sweet, aromatic character of cardamom in this unique breakfast pastry will awaken your spirit and senses!

For the dough

3/4 cup water, at room temperature

1 package (2 1/2 teaspoons) active dry yeast

3 eggs

3 1/2 cups all-purpose flour

1/4 cup sugar

1/2 teaspoon salt

6 tablespoons (3/4 stick) unsalted butter

1 tablespoon minced lemon zest

2 teaspoons ground cardamom

1/2 cup (1 stick) unsalted butter, softened

For the filling

1 large mango

2 tablespoons brown sugar

1 teaspoon vanilla extract

For the glaze

1/4 cup orange marmalade or apple jelly

1 tablespoon water

To prepare the dough, pour the water into a mixing bowl, sprinkle in the yeast, and allow to sit for 2 minutes. Add the eggs, flour, sugar, salt, 6 tablespoons butter, lemon zest, and cardamom. Mix with a dough hook attachment for 5 to 6 minutes, until dough is elastic and smooth. Transfer to a bowl that has been brushed with vegetable oil and cover with plastic wrap. Allow to rest and rise for 30 minutes.

Turn the dough onto a floured work surface, dust with flour, and roll into a rectangle approximately 12 to 18 inches long. Press the 1/2 cup softened butter onto one-half the length of the rectangle, leaving a 1-inch border along the edges. Fold the other half of the rectangle over the buttered half, and pinch at the seams all the way around to seal the butter inside. Roll the dough to about 14×6-inch rectangle. Fold both ends of the rectangle inward, leaving a 1-inch space between the ends in the center. Fold in half, like closing a book. Wrap the dough and refrigerate for 1 hour or overnight.

Preheat oven to 400°F. On a floured work surface, roll the dough into a 14-inch square approximately 1/4 to 3/8 inch thick. Allow to rest for 5 minutes. Using a pastry wheel Doso knife, cut the square into approximately 1 1/2-inch-wide strips. Hold the end of one strip while twisting the other end, until the strip is completely twisted. Pick up the end you were twisting and coil it around the other end. Tuck the end of the strip underneath the coil. Repeat with each strip, and transfer them to a parchment-lined cookie sheet, at least 2 1/2 inches apart. Cover with plastic wrap and allow to rise in a warm place (74° to 80°F), such as the stove top above the warm oven, for 30 to 45 minutes.

Peel the mango with a potato peeler and trim the flesh from the center pit with a sharp knife. Cut the fruit into approximate 1/2-inch cubes and place in a bowl. Toss with the brown sugar and vanilla. With wet fingers, make a well in the center of each coiled Danish. Spoon some mango filling into each.

Bake at 400°F for 16 to 18 minutes, until golden brown. Set aside and allow to cool. While cooling, heat the marmalade or apple jelly with the tablespoon of water in a small sauté pan over medium heat. When it is thinned and runny, brush the jelly glaze over the Danish. Serve.

Allspice Tangerine Brazil Nut Danish

MAKES 8 TO 10 DANISH

I think allspice is the ultimate seasoning for citrus. The pungent, floral character of allspice combined with the tangy, tart, and piquant nature of citrus is a perfect marriage of flavor. The addition of roasted Brazil nuts makes these Danish a hearty partner for a double espresso or strong coffee.

For the dough

3/4 cup milk, at room temperature

1 package (2 1/2 teaspoons) active dry yeast

3 eggs

3 1/2 cups all-purpose flour

1/4 cup sugar

1/2 teaspoon salt

1 tablespoon minced tangerine zest (or substitute orange zest)

2 teaspoons ground allspice

1/2 cup (1 stick) unsalted butter, softened

For the filling

1/2 cup Brazil nuts, lightly crushed

5 tangerines (or substitute oranges)

1 teaspoon ground allspice

1 tablespoon powdered sugar

For the glaze

1/4 cup orange marmalade

1 tablespoon water

To prepare the dough, pour the milk into a mixing bowl, sprinkle in the yeast and allow to sit for 2 minutes. Add the eggs, flour, sugar, salt, tangerine zest, and allspice. Mix with the dough hook attachment for 5 to 6 minutes, until dough is elastic and smooth. Transfer to a bowl that has been brushed with vegetable oil and cover with plastic wrap. Allow to rest and rise for 30 minutes.

Turn the dough onto a floured work surface, dust with flour, and roll into a rectangle approximately 12 to 18 inches long.

Press the 1/2 cup softened butter onto one-half the length of the rectangle, leaving a 1-inch border along the edges. Fold the other half of the rectangle over the buttered half, and pinch at the seams all the way around to seal the butter inside. Roll the dough to about 14×6-inch rectangle. Fold both ends of the rectangle inward, leaving a 1-inch space between the ends in the center. Fold in half, like closing a book. Wrap the dough and refrigerate for 1 hour or overnight.

To prepare the filling, preheat oven to 350°F. Place the Brazil nuts on a cookie sheet and roast in the oven for 14 to 16 minutes. Remove from oven and set aside to cool. When cool to the touch, remove any remaining papery covering and lightly crush the nuts.

On a floured work surface, roll the dough into an approximate 8×12-inch rectangle. Juice one of the tangerines and set aside. Peel the remaining 4 tangerines and break them into wedges. Brush the tangerine juice over the rectangle of dough, and evenly sift the allspice and powdered sugar over the top. Sprinkle the crushed roasted Brazil nuts over the rectangle. Place the tangerine wedges along the bottom of the rectangle, about 1 to 2 inches from the edge. Roll the edge over the tangerines and continue rolling, stretching slightly on the ends to create a tight roll. Using a serrated knife, cut crosswise into 1 1/2- to 2-inch slices. Place each slice flat on a parchment-lined cookie sheet, at least 2 1/2 inches apart, tucking the loose end underneath the Danish. Cover with plastic wrap and allow to rise in a warm place (74° to 80°F), such as on the stove top over the warm oven, for 30 to 45 minutes.

Preheat the oven to 400°F and bake the Danish for 16 to 18 minutes, until golden brown. Set aside and allow to cool. While cooling, heat the orange marmalade with the tablespoon of water in a small sauté pan over medium heat. When it is thinned and runny, brush the jelly glaze over the Danish. Serve.

Danishes (front to back): Cardamom-Mango, Grapefruit, and Allspice Tangerine Brazil Nut

Brazil Nut–Chocolate Brownies

*MAKES ONE 10×12×2-INCH PAN, OR **12** TO **14** SERVINGS*

Brownies are the quintessential American comfort dessert. Simple to make and always satisfying, their tantalizing aroma fills the kitchen and beckons with rich chocolate anticipation. I think Brazil nuts are one of the best nuts to pair with chocolate. Their earthy, roasted flavor contrasts nicely with smooth, bittersweet chocolate.

1 cup Brazil nuts

4 ounces bittersweet chocolate

6 tablespoons unsalted butter

3 eggs

1 1/2 cups sugar

1/4 teaspoon salt

1 teaspoon vanilla extract

1 cup all-purpose flour

1/2 teaspoon baking soda

Preheat oven to 350°F. Spread the Brazil nuts on a cookie sheet and roast in the oven for 14 to 16 minutes, until golden brown. Remove them from the oven, set aside to cool, and decrease the oven temperature to 325°F. When the nuts are cool enough to handle, turn them out on the work surface and crush them lightly with the side of a chef's knife.

Melt the chocolate and butter together in the top part of a double boiler over hot, but not boiling, water. Remove the bowl from the heat and allow the chocolate to cool.

Using a mixer on high speed, whip together the eggs, sugar, salt, and vanilla extract until lightened and thick. Set aside. In a separate bowl, sift together the flour and baking soda. Whisk the chocolate into the whipped egg mixture, then fold in the sifted flour and roasted nuts until thoroughly combined.

Prepare the baking pan by brushing it with melted butter or vegetable oil and dusting with flour. Pour the brownie batter into the pan and spread evenly with a spatula. Bake on the middle rack of the oven for 1 hour, or until a knife inserted into the center comes out clean. Cool on a rack, cut, and serve.

Cinnamon-Sugar Twists

*MAKES **18** TO **22** TWISTS*

These cinnamon sugar twists are quick and simple and make a perfect snack food or delicious accompaniment to coffee or tea. Frozen puff pastry is available in most supermarkets.

1 sheet puff pastry

2 egg whites

1 tablespoon ground cinnamon

2 tablespoons powdered sugar

Preheat oven to 400°F. Sprinkle the work surface lightly with flour. Roll the puff pastry to a thickness of 1/16 inch. Brush off the excess flour from the pastry and brush the surface of the dough with egg white. Sift together the cinnamon and powdered sugar in a large bowl, and then resift one-half of the mixture over the surface of the dough. Roll the puff pastry sheet onto the rolling pin, turn it over, and roll it out on the work surface so the plain side faces up. Brush this side with egg white and sift the remaining cinnamon-sugar mixture on top. Using a pastry wheel or chef's knife, cut the pastry into 1-inch strips. Hold one end down and twist the other end several times to create a corkscrew shape. Transfer the twists to a parchment-covered or nonstick sheet pan and bake for 12 to 14 minutes, or until golden brown.

Coconut Cream Puffs

*MAKES **12** TO **14** PUFFS*

These cream puffs are miniature versions of coconut cream pie. Get your hammer out of the toolbox and crack open a fresh coconut—it's the only way to enjoy the full flavor of this tropical fruit! Use a peeler or grater to make ribbonlike shavings for the filling and for adorning the tops of the puffs. Baking the shavings on top gives the puffs an attractive rustic appearance and a burst of coconut flavor in the first bite.

For the puffs

1 coconut

1 cup milk

1/4 cup (1/2 stick) unsalted butter

1/4 teaspoon salt

1/2 cup all-purpose flour

2 eggs

For the filling

1 cup milk

2 egg yolks

1/4 cup brown sugar

2 tablespoons all-purpose flour

1/2 cup heavy cream

Powdered sugar for dusting

To prepare the puffs, preheat oven to 375°F. Poke a hole in the "eye" of the coconut and drain the water into a bowl, reserving it for another use. Roast the whole coconut in the oven at 375°F for 20 minutes. Remove the coconut and allow it to cool. Increase the oven temperature to 425°F. Crack the cooled coconut on a hard surface and pry the flesh from the shell with a large spoon. Use a peeler to make 1 cup of coconut shavings from the white flesh.

In a medium saucepan, combine the milk, butter, and salt and place over medium heat. When mixture simmers and butter is completely melted, whisk in the flour. Continue stirring over the heat for 1 minute, until the mixture pulls away from the sides of the pot. Remove the pan from the heat and allow to cool for 6 to 8 minutes. Whisk in the eggs one at a time until the mixture is smooth and shiny. Using either a piping bag with a large plain tip or a spoon, create 2-inch mounds of cream puff dough on a parchment-lined cookie sheet. Sprinkle each mound with some of the coconut shavings. Bake for 14 to 16 minutes, then reduce heat to 375°F and bake another 8 to 10 minutes. Remove from oven and allow to cool on a rack.

For the filling, using a hand-held grater or food processor, grate 1 cup of the remaining coconut meat. Combine the milk and coconut in a saucepan and bring to a simmer over medium heat. While waiting for this to simmer, combine the egg yolks and brown sugar in a mixing bowl and whisk together. Add the flour and whisk thoroughly. Continue whisking while pouring half of the simmering milk mixture into the yolk mixture. Then whisk the entire yolk mixture into the remaining hot milk in the saucepan, and return to medium heat, stirring constantly. When the mixture begins to boil, stir continuously for one minute past the boiling point. Remove from heat, pour into a bowl, and gently press a piece of plastic wrap directly onto the surface of the pastry cream. Cool the mixture by placing the pan on ice or in the freezer. Whip the cream until stiff and fold it into the cooled coconut pastry cream until smooth.

Slice each baked puff in half crosswise and fill the bottom half with a spoon of the coconut filling. Place the tops on the cream, dust with powdered sugar, and serve.

He who plants a coconut tree plants vessels and clothing, food and drink, a habitation for himself and a heritage for his children.

—SOUTH SEAS PROVERB

Chocolate-Pecan Muffins

MAKES ***6*** *TO* ***8*** *LARGE MUFFINS,* ***10*** *TO* ***12*** *MEDIUM MUFFINS, OR* ***18*** *TO* ***24*** *MINIMUFFINS*

Muffins are one of the most simple and widely enjoyed forms of breakfast bread. This recipe is especially nice for a holiday morning when feeding family and friends. Use a high-quality dark unsweetened cocoa powder to make chocolate muffins that are not overly sweet and can be enjoyed for breakfast or at any time of day with coffee, tea, or foaming cappuccino.

1 cup pecans

13/4 cups all-purpose flour

3/4 cup cocoa powder

1 cup sugar

2 teaspoons baking powder

1 teaspoon baking soda

1/2 teaspoon salt

1/2 teaspoon ground cinnamon

1 tablespoon minced orange zest

1/2 cup chocolate chips

1/2 cup canola or other vegetable oil

1 cup milk

2 eggs

Preheat oven to 350°F. Spread the pecans on a cookie sheet and roast in the oven for 14 to 16 minutes, until golden brown. Remove the nuts from the oven, set aside to cool, and increase the oven temperature to 375°F.

Sift the flour, cocoa powder, sugar, baking powder, baking soda, salt and cinnamon together in a large bowl. Stir in the roasted pecans, orange zest, and chocolate chips. Set aside. In a separate large bowl, whisk together the oil, milk, and eggs. Using a spoon, fold the dry ingredients into the wet mixture until just combined. Do not overmix. When making muffins, it's good to have some small unmixed chunks of flour visible in the batter. This creates a lighter texture in the baked muffins.

Prepare your muffin pans by brushing with oil or butter and dusting with flour. Divide the batter among the muffin molds, filling to the top. Bake for 20 to 30 minutes on the middle rack of the oven, or until a knife inserted into the center of a muffin comes out clean. Reduce the baking time by 5 minutes for minimuffins or increase by 5 minutes for large muffins. Remove from the oven and allow to cool for several minutes in the pan before turning out on a wire rack.

Macadamia–Dark Rum Muffins

Rum is made with fermented sugar cane, and has long been an important product of the Caribbean. Its true tropical spirit combined with rich macadamias creates a robust and adventurous muffin. Enjoy these muffins at an outdoor breakfast on a warm morning.

1 cup macadamia nuts

2 1/2 cups all-purpose flour

2 teaspoons baking powder

1 teaspoon salt

1 teaspoon ground allspice

1/4 cup (1/2 stick) unsalted butter, melted

3/4 cup dark brown sugar

1/4 cup canola or other vegetable oil

1 egg, beaten

1/4 cup milk

1/2 cup dark rum

Preheat oven to 350°F. Spread the macadamias on a cookie sheet and roast in the oven for 14 to 16 minutes, until golden brown. Remove them from the oven, set aside to cool, and increase the oven temperature to 375°F. When the nuts are cool enough to handle, turn them out on a work surface and lightly chop.

Sift the flour, baking powder, salt, and allspice together in a large bowl. Stir in the roasted macadamia nuts. Set aside. In a separate large bowl, whisk together all the remaining ingredients. Using a spoon, fold the dry ingredients into the wet mixture until just combined. Do not overmix. When making muffins, it's good to have some small unmixed chunks of flour visible in the batter. This creates a lighter texture in the baked muffins.

Prepare muffin pans by greasing with oil or butter and dusting with flour. Divide the batter among the muffin molds, filling to the top. Bake for 20 to 30 minutes on the middle rack of the oven, or until a knife inserted into the center of a muffin comes out clean. Reduce the baking time by 5 minutes for minimuffins or increase by 5 minutes for large muffins. Remove from the oven and allow to cool for several minutes in the pan before turning out on a wire rack.

Asian Sesame Doughnuts

MAKES *12* TO *14* DOUGHNUTS

Doughnuts are an American version of the French beignet, or sweet fritters, which are also very popular in New Orleans. This recipe is inspired by Asian influences of fresh gingerroot combined with sesame, both products of tropical and subtropical climates. Enjoy these Zen-like minimalist doughnuts with a cup of green, black, or jasmine tea.

2 tablespoons unsalted butter

1/2 cup sugar

1/4 cup honey

1 egg

1 tablespoon finely grated gingerroot

2 tablespoons water

2 1/4 cups all-purpose flour

1 teaspoon baking powder

1/2 cup sesame seeds

3 cups peanut oil or other vegetable oil for frying

Powdered sugar for dusting

Cream the butter, sugar, and honey together in a mixer using the paddle attachment. Add the egg, ginger, and water and beat at high speed until light and fluffy.

In a separate bowl, sift together the flour and baking powder. Work this dry mixture into the wet mixture by hand, kneading the dough until soft and well combined.

On a floured work surface, use your hands to roll the dough to cylindrical ropelike shape with a diameter of 1 to 1 1/2 inches and a length of approximately 18 inches. Cut into 1 1/2-inch-long pieces. Roll each piece between the palms of your hands to form round balls. Dip each ball in water and roll in sesame seeds.

Heat the frying oil in a wok or heavy-bottomed pan over medium heat until sizzling. The oil will be hot enough if a small piece of dough dropped into it sizzles and rises to the top. Reduce the heat to low. Cook several doughnuts at a time, turning occasionally, for 5 to 6 minutes. Remove from oil using a slotted spoon and drain on a paper bag or paper towels. Allow to cool, sprinkle with powdered sugar, and enjoy.

Asian Sesame Doughnuts

Pistachio Honey Cardamom Doughnuts

MAKES 12 TO 14 DOUGHNUTS

These doughnuts recall deep-fried dough snacks sold from street carts or in the outdoor markets, or souks, of North Africa. Pistachios, honey, and cardamom are all widely used ingredients in North African, Near Eastern, Mediterranean, and Indian cuisines. Enjoy these aromatic doughnuts in the afternoon with tea or coffee. For a special treat, serve them with Moroccan mint tea, anisette-spiked coffee, or cardamom-flavored tea or coffee.

For the doughnuts

1 cup milk, at room temperature

1 tablespoon (1 package) active dry yeast

1/4 cup honey

1/4 cup (1/2 stick) unsalted butter, melted

3 eggs

3 1/3 cups all-purpose flour

1/2 teaspoon salt

2 teaspoons ground cardamom

1/2 cup pistachios

3 cups peanut oil or other vegetable oil for frying

For the glaze

1/2 cup pistachios

1/4 cup honey

2 tablespoons water

1/2 cup powdered sugar

For the doughnuts, pour the milk into a large mixing bowl, sprinkle in the yeast and allow to sit 2 minutes. Add the honey, butter, eggs, flour, salt, cardamom and pistachios. Mix with a dough hook attachment for 5 to 6 minutes, until a soft dough has formed. Cover with plastic wrap and allow to rest and rise for 30 minutes.

Remove the dough from the bowl and cut it into approximate 2-inch-diameter pieces. Roll each piece between the palms of your hands to form round balls, then use your fingers to poke a hole in the center of each. Place the doughnuts on a lightly floured cookie sheet. Cover them with plastic wrap and allow to rest and rise another 15 minutes.

Heat the frying oil in a wok or heavy-bottomed pan over medium heat until sizzling. The oil will be hot enough if a small piece of dough dropped into it sizzles and rises to the top. Reduce the heat to low. Cook several doughnuts at a time, turning occasionally, for 4 to 6 minutes. Remove from oil using a slotted spoon and drain on a paper bag or paper towels. Allow to cool.

Preheat oven to 350°F. To prepare the glaze, spread the pistachios on a dry cookie sheet and roast them in the oven for 8 to 10 minutes, just until they begin to brown. Remove them from the oven and turn them out onto a cutting board. Lightly chop the nuts with a chef's knife. In a small bowl, whisk together the honey, water, and powdered sugar. Brush the glaze over the doughnuts and sprinkle with the chopped pistachios. Serve.

Lemon-Pecan Coffee Cake

*MAKES ONE 10×14×2-INCH CAKE, OR **12** TO **14** SERVINGS*

Pecans are the nut of a large hickory tree that is widely grown throughout Mexico and the southern United States. One of Donna's fondest childhood memories is gathering fallen pecans from the ground beneath a large pecan tree behind her grandmother's North Carolina home. Coffee cake's light interior and brown sugar crumbly topping are always a delicious breakfast treat. In this recipe, the cake is flavored with lemon juice and roasted pecans.

For the cake

1 cup pecans

1 cup canola oil

3 eggs

1/4 cup fresh lemon juice

1/2 teaspoon vanilla extract

1 1/2 cups sugar

2 1/4 cups all-purpose flour

1 teaspoon baking powder

1 teaspoon baking soda

1 teaspoon salt

1/2 teaspoon ground cinnamon

For the crumb topping

1/2 cup (1 stick) unsalted butter, chopped into 1/2-inch pieces

1 cup dark brown sugar

3/4 cup all-purpose flour

1 tablespoon lemon zest, chopped fine

Powdered sugar for dusting

Preheat oven to 350°F. Spread the pecans on a dry cookie sheet and roast them in the oven for 12 to 14 minutes, or until golden brown. Remove them from the oven and set aside to cool.

In a large mixing bowl, whisk together the oil, eggs, lemon juice, and vanilla extract. Whisk in the sugar. In a separate bowl, sift together the flour, baking powder, baking soda, salt, and cinnamon. Stir in the pecans. Stir the dry ingredients into the wet ingredients until well combined. Set aside.

To prepare the crumb topping, using the paddle attachment on a mixer, combine the chopped butter, brown sugar, flour, and lemon zest for the topping. Mix on low speed until the butter breaks into small bits and the mixture appears crumbly. Set aside.

Prepare a 10×14×2-inch pan by brushing with butter or oil and dusting with flour. Pour the batter into the pan and spread evenly with a spatula. Sprinkle the crumb topping evenly over the top of the batter. Bake for approximately 45 to 50 minutes. Allow to cool in the pan. Dust lightly with powdered sugar and cut into desired servings.

> *Desolate lemons, hold*
> *tight, in your bowl of earth,*
> *the light to your bitter flesh,*
>
> *let a lemon glare*
> *be all your armour*
> *this naked Sunday . . .*
> —DEREK WALCOTT, "SUNDAY LEMONS"

Asian Pear–Banana Coffee Cake

*MAKES ONE 10×10×2-INCH PAN, OR **12** TO **14** SERVINGS*

I think round, crisp Asian pears resemble apples more than pears, but their luscious, juicy character puts them in a class by themselves. Chunks of Asian pear and banana baked in this cake make it especially moist and fruity, and are complemented by the robust flavors of orange zest, almonds, and rum.

1 cup (2 sticks) unsalted butter

1 cup plus 2 tablespoons sugar

1 teaspoon vanilla extract

1/4 teaspoon salt

2 tablespoons dark rum (optional), or brandy or bourbon

3 eggs

13/4 cups all-purpose flour

1 teaspoon baking powder

1 teaspoon ground allspice

1/2 cup almonds, finely ground in a food processor

1 tablespoon minced orange zest

1 Asian pear, cored and chopped into 1/2-inch pieces

1 banana, peeled and sliced 1/4 inch thick

Powdered sugar for dusting

Preheat oven to 350°F. Using the whip attachment on a mixer, begin whipping the butter. Add the sugar, vanilla, salt, and rum and whip until light and creamy, occasionally scraping the sides of the bowl with a rubber spatula. Add the eggs one at a time, and continue whipping until smooth.

In a separate bowl, sift together the flour, baking powder, and allspice. Stir in the ground almonds and orange zest. Fold the dry ingredients into the wet ingredients until well combined. Fold in the Asian pear and banana pieces.

Prepare a 10×10×2-inch pan by brushing with oil or butter and dusting with flour. Pour the batter into the pan and spread evenly with a spatula. Bake for approximately 1 hour, or until a knife inserted in the center of the bread comes out clean. Allow to cool on a rack. Dust with powdered sugar and cut into desired sizes.

Bohicon Banana Breakfast Bread

MAKES ONE 8×4×4-INCH LOAF, OR 10 SERVINGS

This bread is named for Bohicon, a bustling market town in Bénin, West Africa. When I lived in Bénin, Bohicon was the first stop on the train line between my village and the city of Cotonou where fresh-picked, baby bananas were available. Upon pulling into the station, train passengers eagerly leaned out the high windows to purchase bunches of bananas from market women who balanced overflowing trays of them on their heads. Bohicon's baby bananas were some of the best I've ever tasted, plump and sweet with very thin skins. If you can't find baby bananas, try using flavorful red bananas.

1 cup cashews

1/2 cup (1 stick) unsalted butter

3/4 cup dark brown sugar

3 bananas, very ripe and mashed with a fork

3 eggs

1/4 cup milk

1/2 teaspoon vanilla extract

1 cup whole wheat flour

3/4 cup all-purpose flour

2 teaspoons baking powder

1/4 teaspoon salt

Preheat oven to 350°F. Spread the cashews on a cookie sheet and roast them in the oven for 14 to 16 minutes, or until golden brown. Remove them from the oven and set aside to cool.

Using the whip attachment on a mixer, whip the butter and brown sugar until pale in color and light in consistency. Add the banana mash and continue whipping on low speed until well mixed. Add the eggs one at a time, then the milk and vanilla extract, and continue whipping until well combined. Set aside. In a separate bowl, stir together the two types of flour, baking powder, salt, and cashews. Fold the dry mixture into the wet mixture until combined.

Prepare the loaf pan by brushing with oil or butter and dusting with flour. Pour the batter into the pan and spread evenly with a spatula. Bake for approximately 1 hour 15 minutes, or until a knife inserted in the center of the bread comes out clean. Cool on a rack, slice, and serve.

Golden Raisin–Clove Bread

*MAKES ONE 8×4×4-INCH LOAF, OR **10** SERVINGS*

Golden raisins, or sultanas, are made by drying green grapes in the shade. They're produced in southern Africa, South America, Mexico, and other grape-growing countries including the United States and France. The combination of golden raisins with the pungent clove makes a comforting cold-weather or holiday breakfast bread.

3/4 cup (1 1/2 sticks) unsalted butter

1/2 cup sugar

2 tablespoons dark molasses

1 tablespoon minced lemon zest

4 eggs

1 teaspoon vanilla extract

1 tablespoon brandy (optional)

1 cup all-purpose flour

1/4 cup whole wheat flour

1/2 cup cornstarch

1 teaspoon baking powder

1/2 teaspoon salt

1 teaspoon ground cloves

1 cup golden raisins, plumped in 1/2 cup hot water
   for 10 to 12 minutes

1/2 cup walnuts, lightly roasted (optional)

Preheat oven to 350°F. In a mixer, whip the butter, sugar, molasses, and lemon zest. Add the eggs one at a time, continuing to mix on medium speed. Add the vanilla and brandy. Set aside.

Sift together the flours, cornstarch, baking powder, salt, and cloves in a medium-sized bowl. Stir the dry ingredients into the egg mixture until well combined. Stir in the raisins and walnuts.

Prepare an 8×4×4-inch loaf pan by brushing with butter or oil and dusting with flour. Turn the batter into the pan and spread evenly with a spatula. Bake for 60 to 70 minutes, or until a paring knife inserted in the center comes out clean. Cool the bread in the pan for 20 minutes. Remove from pan, slice, and serve.

Peanut-Allspice Bread

*MAKES ONE 8×4×4-INCH LOAF, OR **10** SERVINGS*

In this recipe, allspice enhances the peanut flavor and also matches well with the chocolate chips, should you include them. Be sure to use only freshly ground peanut butter, which can be bought in bulk in natural food stores, for its strong, roasted character.

4 eggs

3/4 cup dark brown sugar

1 1/2 cups all-purpose flour

1 teaspoon baking powder

1/4 teaspoon salt

1 teaspoon ground allspice

1 cup freshly ground (unhomogenized) peanut butter

1/4 cup (1/2 stick) unsalted butter, melted

1/2 cup chocolate chips (optional)

Preheat oven to 375°F. Using the whip attachment for your mixer, whip the eggs and brown sugar at high speed for 6 to 7 minutes, or until light and creamy. Set aside.

Sift together the flour, baking powder, salt, and allspice in a medium-sized bowl. Set aside.

Turn the peanut butter into a large mixing bowl with the melted butter and stir until well combined and the peanut butter has softened. Fold one-third of the whipped eggs into the peanut butter, then fold in one third of the flour mixture. Alternate folding in the remaining eggs and flour until all the ingredients are combined and mixture is smooth.

Prepare an 8×4×4-inch loaf pan by brushing with butter or oil and dusting with flour. Turn the batter into the pan and spread evenly with a spatula. Bake for 55 to 60 minutes, or until a paring knife inserted in the center comes out clean. Cool the bread in the pan for 20 minutes. Remove from pan, slice, and serve.

Persimmon-Date Bread

MAKES TWO 8×4×4-INCH LOAVES, OR 18 TO 20 SERVINGS

The luscious flesh of ripe persimmons, which ranges in color from yellow to deep orange, makes a delicious, moist bread. Be sure the fruit is fully ripe, or it will taste bitter and astringent. The fruity sweetness of persimmons pairs well with dates, which are rich in natural sugars.

31/4 cups all-purpose flour

1/2 cup whole wheat flour

2 teaspoons baking soda

1/2 teaspoon ground cloves

1/2 cup (1 stick) unsalted butter, melted

1/2 cup canola oil

1 cup brown sugar

3 eggs

13/4 cups milk

1 teaspoon vanilla extract

1/2 cup dark molasses

1 cup dates, preferably Medjooli, pitted and lightly chopped

2 ripe persimmons, with center stems and black pits removed, lightly chopped

Preheat oven to 350°F. Sift together the flours, baking soda, and cloves into a mixing bowl. In a separate bowl, whisk together the butter, oil, brown sugar, eggs, milk, vanilla, and molasses until well combined. Fold in the dates and persimmon. Fold the dry ingredients into the wet mixture, until just combined.

Prepare two 8×4×4-inch loaf pans by brushing with butter or oil and dusting with flour. Divide the batter between the two pans and spread evenly with a spatula. Bake for 55 to 65 minutes, or until a paring knife inserted in the center comes out clean. Cool the bread in the pans for 12 to 15 minutes, then turn out onto a wire rack until thoroughly cooled. Slice and serve.

Having planted a banana tree,
I'm a little contemptuous
of the bush clover.

This old village—
Not a single house
without persimmon trees.
—JAPANESE HAIKU BY MATSUO BASHO (1644–94)

Zesty Lemon-Almond Bread

*MAKES TWO 8×4×4-INCH LOAVES, OR **18** TO **20** SERVINGS*

This recipe is an adaptation of a bread my father made in his bakery in New England. Enjoy this bread with lemon tea, iced tea, or freshly squeezed lemonade. It can also be served as dessert, topped with a dollop of whipped cream or fresh fruit.

1 cup sliced almonds

1/2 cup minced lemon zest (about 4 lemons)

1/2 cup sugar

1/2 cup lemon juice

3 cups all-purpose flour

1/2 teaspoon salt

2 teaspoons baking powder

1/4 cup sugar

2 eggs

1 cup (2 sticks) unsalted butter, melted

3/4 cup milk

Preheat oven to 350°F. Spread the sliced almonds on a cookie sheet and roast in the oven for 14 to 16 minutes, until golden brown. Remove the nuts from the oven and set aside to cool. Leave the oven temperature at 350°F.

Combine the lemon zest, sugar, and juice in a small saucepan over medium heat. Bring mixture to a boil, then reduce heat and simmer for 12 to 14 minutes or until the lemon zest becomes translucent. Set aside to cool.

Sift together the flour, salt, baking powder, and sugar, and stir in the almonds. In a separate bowl, whisk together the eggs, butter, milk, and water. Stir the dry ingredients into the wet mixture, gently folding until just combined.

Prepare two 8×4×4-inch loaf pans by brushing with butter or oil and dusting with flour. Divide the batter between the two pans and spread evenly with a spatula. Bake for 60 to 70 minutes, or until a paring knife inserted in the center comes out clean. Cool the bread in the pans for 12 to 15 minutes, then turn out onto a wire rack until thoroughly cooled. Slice and serve.

Pineapple-Rum Bread

*MAKES TWO 8×4×4-INCH LOAVES, OR **18** TO **20** SERVINGS*

The flavors of this bread echo a tropical fruit cocktail enjoyed in the warm, coastal breezes of the Caribbean. Baked with pineapple rings adorning the top, this attractive bread is perfect for Sunday brunch or special occasions. Choose golden and yellow-toned pineapples to ensure sweet ripeness.

1 pineapple

3 cups all-purpose flour

3/4 cup sugar

1/2 teaspoon salt

2 teaspoons baking powder

3/4 cup (1 1/2 sticks) unsalted butter, melted

1/2 cup dark brown sugar

3 eggs

1/2 cup milk

1/2 cup dark rum

Preheat oven to 350°F. Trim the top and bottom off the pineapple and slice off the skin, from top to bottom, working around the fruit until finished. Cut the pineapple in half crosswise. Using an apple corer, remove the core from each half. Chop one half into 1/2-inch chucks and cut the other half into 1/4-inch-thick round slices.

Sift together the flour, sugar, salt, and baking powder in a medium-sized bowl. In a separate bowl, whisk together the butter, brown sugar, eggs, milk, and rum. Fold the dry ingredients into the wet ingredients, then fold in the pineapple chunks.

Prepare two 8×4×4-inch loaf pans by brushing with butter or oil and dusting with flour. Divide the batter between the two pans and spread evenly with a spatula. Lay the pineapple slices on top of the batter. Bake for 60 to 70 minutes, or until a paring knife inserted in the center comes out clean. Cool the bread in the pans for 12 to 15 minutes, then turn out onto a wire rack until thoroughly cooled. Slice and serve.

Papaya Lime Cracked Pepper Bread

*MAKES TWO 8×4×4-INCH LOAVES, OR **18** TO **20** SERVINGS*

This unusual bread sports a flavor combination I love: papaya and lime. I like to add black pepper, as its heat and zip balances out the sweet nature of papaya. This bread is great for picnics, or served with meals that feature grilled fish or shellfish.

2 1/2 cups all-purpose flour

1 cup whole wheat flour

1 cup dark brown sugar

1/2 teaspoon salt

1 teaspoon baking soda

1 teaspoon baking powder

1 1/2 teaspoons medium ground black pepper

1 papaya

3/4 cup (1 1/2 sticks) unsalted butter, softened

1/4 cup honey

1/4 cup plain yogurt

1/4 cup lime juice

2 eggs

Preheat oven to 350°F. Sift together the flours, brown sugar, salt, baking soda, and baking powder. Stir in the black pepper and set aside. Peel the papaya, scrape out the seeds with a spoon, and cut the fruit into 1/2-inch chunks. Set aside.

Using the whisk attachment on a mixer, cream the butter and honey. Add the yogurt and lime juice and whisk until smooth. Add the eggs one at a time, and continue whisking until smooth. Fold in the dry mixture and the papaya chunks, and stir until just combined.

Prepare two 8×4×4-inch loaf pans by brushing with butter or oil and dusting with flour. Divide the batter between the pans and spread it evenly with a spatula. Bake for 60 to 70 minutes, or until a paring knife inserted in the center comes out clean. Cool the bread in the pans for 12 to 15 minutes, then turn out onto a wire rack until thoroughly cooled. Slice and serve.

Persian Date Crumble

*MAKES ONE 10-INCH ROUND PAN, OR **8** TO **10** SERVINGS*

Dates originated in Persia. Crumbles are old-fashioned, rustic American home-style desserts related to crisps, brown betties, and buckles. This crumble uses a filling that requires no additional sweetener because of the fruit's natural sugars.

1 cup (2 sticks) unsalted butter

1 cup sugar

1 egg

Zest of 1 orange

3 1/2 cups all-purpose flour

1 teaspoon baking powder

1/2 teaspoon salt

3 cups dates, pitted and lightly chopped

1/2 cup water

1/2 cup shelled pistachios, crushed with the side of a chef's knife

Powdered sugar for decoration

Preheat oven to 375°F. Using the paddle attachment on a mixer, cream the butter and sugar. Add the egg and orange zest. In a separate bowl, sift together the flour, baking powder, and salt. Work this dry mixture into the wet mixture on low speed, until well combined and crumbly in appearance.

Prepare a 10-inch round cake pan by brushing with butter or oil and dusting with flour. Press one half of the crumb mixture into the bottom of the cake pan, covering the bottom and sides so that it has a 1-inch-high rim.

Combine the dates and water in a saucepan and place over medium heat. Simmer for 8 to 10 minutes, stirring periodically. Spoon the softened date mixture into the crumb crust, sprinkle with the pistachios, and pack the remaining crumb mixture on top.

Bake for 55 to 60 minutes, or until browned. Cool for 10 minutes in the pan, then remove from the pan and cool on a rack. Sprinkle powdered sugar over the cooled crumble and serve.

the 18th and 19th centuries, it was believed to have medicinal properties and was sold by apothecaries and pharmacists. It was also considered an aphrodisiac in both France and England. Throughout much of the 18th century, chocolate was branded as a threat to women's virtue in England due to popular fears of its seductive qualities leading them to abandon norms of female chastity. But these myths dissipated by the end of that century, and consumption of chocolate grew widespread among all European classes.

Some of the chocolate recipes in this chapter are based on European ganache-filled chocolates, invented by the Swiss in 1913. Dipped in tempered chocolate to create a shiny, hard coating, they have soft chocolate centers infused with flavors of tropical spices like cardamom and canela cinnamon. Other recipes pair chocolate with tropical fruits, like bananas or kumquats. For the simplest preparations, tropical and subtropical fruits, like starfruits and kiwis, are dipped in bittersweet or white chocolate. You'll also enjoy the simple candy recipes in this chapter—candies don't have to be difficult to make in order to be delicious! These homemade jellies, nougats, and marzipans make use of exotic tropical products, like persimmons, tamarillos, and plantains. These candy recipes are short on method and long on flavor. In only a few quick steps, you'll have tiny tempting treasures bursting with the flavor of the tropics!

(Clockwise from top): Brazil Nut Chocolate-Chip Cookies, Nutmeg-Orange Cookies, Kuli Kuli Peanut Sticks, Aniseed Cookies, and Pistachio-Chocolate Cookies

Brazil Nut Chocolate-Chip Cookies

*MAKES **25** TO **30** COOKIES*

Chocolate-chip cookies were invented in 1933 by Ruth Graves Wakefield, innkeeper of the Toll House Inn in Whitman, Massachusetts. Her spontaneous experiment of dropping pieces of semisweet chocolate bars into cookie batter was the beginning of an American tradition. Now you can surprise everyone, like Ruth did, by studding traditional chocolate chip cookies with untraditional Brazil nuts!

1/4 cup (1/2 stick) unsalted butter, softened

3/4 cup sugar

3/4 cup dark brown sugar

2 eggs

1/2 teaspoon vanilla extract

2 1/4 cups all-purpose flour

1 teaspoon baking soda

1/2 teaspoon salt

3/4 cup bittersweet chocolate chips (or use semisweet chips)

1 cup shelled Brazil nuts, lightly crushed with the side of a knife

Preheat oven to 350°F. Using a mixer, cream the butter with the sugar and brown sugar. While continuing to whip, add the eggs one at a time at 15-second intervals. Add the vanilla extract and whip until well mixed. In a separate bowl, sift together the flour, baking soda, and salt. With the mixer on low speed, add the dry ingredients to the wet mixture one cup at a time. Scrape the sides of the bowl with a spatula, and continue mixing until the dough is well combined and smooth. Add the chocolate chips and crushed Brazil nuts and mix on low speed just enough to distribute them evenly throughout the dough.

Grease a nonstick cookie sheet. Drop the dough on the pan in 2-tablespoon portions at least 2 inches apart. Bake for 15 to 17 minutes, or until the edges of the cookies are lightly browning. Remove from oven and allow to cool on the pan or on a wire rack. Store sealed in an airtight container.

Kuli Kuli Peanut Sticks

*MAKES **20** TO **25** STICKS*

These kuli kuli peanut treats are popular snacks in West Africa, where market women roll out sticklike forms of freshly ground peanut butter and fry them in kettles over open fires. Packed with peanut protein, they're an excellent source of energy for midmorning or -afternoon, or while engaging in any kind of outdoor activity. They're also simply delicious snacks for any time!

2 cups freshly ground (unhomogenized) peanut butter

1/4 cup sugar

1 1/4 cups all-purpose flour

1/2 teaspoon salt

3 cups peanut oil or other vegetable oil for frying

In a mixer, cream the peanut butter and sugar on low speed. Add the flour and salt and continue mixing until a medium stiff dough forms.

Turn the dough out onto a lightly floured work surface and cut it into pieces approximately the size of walnuts. Roll the lumps of dough into snakelike strips with the palm of your hand, tapering the ends to points.

Heat the oil to approximately 350°F over medium heat, then reduce the heat to low to maintain a steady temperature. The oil should be ready when a small piece of dough dropped into it bubbles vigorously and immediately rises to the surface. Fry several kuli kulis at a time for about 3 minutes. Drain on paper towels and allow to cool before serving.

Nutmeg-Orange Cookies

MAKES *25* TO *30* COOKIES

The pairing of orange with nutmeg is a traditional fruit-spice flavor combination that never fails. The pungent, numbing quality of nutmeg accents and enhances the bright, sweet acidic nature of orange. These flavors rekindle memories of winter holidays, a perfect time for you to bake these cookies. Enjoy them while making merry with a tall glass of eggnog sprinkled with ground nutmeg!

1/2 cup (1 stick) unsalted butter

1/2 cup sugar

1/4 cup dark brown sugar

1/4 cup orange juice

1/4 cup orange liqueur, such as Grand Marnier or Cointreau, or brandy

Zest of 1 orange

1 egg white

2 cups all-purpose flour

1/2 teaspoon baking soda

1 cup finely ground almonds (use a food processor)

1 tablespoon ground nutmeg

Preheat oven to 350°F. Using a mixer, cream the butter with the sugar and brown sugar. Slowly add the orange juice, orange liqueur, and orange zest and mix until well combined. Add the egg white and mix for another 30 seconds. In a separate bowl, sift together the flour and baking soda.

Stir the ground almonds and nutmeg into the dry ingredients. With the mixer on low speed, add the dry ingredients to the wet mixture one cup at a time. Scrape the sides of the bowl with a spatula, and continue mixing until the dough is well combined and smooth. Turn the dough out of the mixing bowl onto the work surface and use your hands to form it into a bricklike shape. Wrap it in plastic wrap and chill in the refrigerator for at least 20 minutes.

Unwrap the chilled dough and place it onto a well-floured work surface. Sprinkle it with flour and use a rolling pin to roll it to 1/4 inch thickness. Cut desired shapes out of the dough and place them 1/2 inch apart on a greased nonstick cookie sheet. Bake for 18 to 22 minutes or until lightly browning on the edges. Remove from oven and allow to cool on the pan or on a wire rack. Store sealed in an airtight container.

He's of the colour of nutmeg.
And of the heat of ginger.
—WILLIAM SHAKESPEARE, *KING HENRY V* 3.6

Pistachio-Chocolate Cookies

*MAKES **20** TO **25** COOKIES*

Chocolate and pistachio are two rich, delicious flavors that pair perfectly. These soft-centered chocolate cookies will be gobbled up so quickly you may want to double the recipe! They're especially luscious when served warm and chewy, straight from the oven.

1 cup shelled pistachios

8 ounces bittersweet chocolate (or use semisweet)

1/2 cup (1 stick) unsalted butter

2 eggs

3/4 cup sugar

1/4 cup all-purpose flour

1 tablespoon finely ground coffee beans (or use 2 teaspoons instant coffee or espresso)

1 teaspoon baking powder

1/4 teaspoon salt

Preheat oven to 350°F. Spread the pistachios on a dry cookie sheet and roast in the oven for 14 to 16 minutes. Set aside to cool and reduce oven temperature to 325°F.

Melt the chocolate and butter in a double boiler, or a bowl set over a pot of hot water. Whisk in the eggs until smooth. In a separate bowl, sift together the sugar, flour, coffee, baking powder, and salt. Stir the dry ingredients into the chocolate mixture until thoroughly combined. Add the roasted pistachios and mix until they are evenly distributed throughout the dough.

Grease a nonstick cookie sheet. Drop the dough by spoonfuls at least 2 inches apart on the pan and bake for 14 to 16 minutes, or until the cookies puff up and the tops of them crack. Remove from oven and allow to cool on the pan or on a wire rack. Store sealed in an airtight container.

Cinnamon Biscuit Cookies

*MAKES **20** TO **25** COOKIES*

These cookies are just like miniature cinnamon breakfast biscuits, with a pleasantly light and airy texture. They're perfect as a simple dessert with bowls of fresh cut tropical fruit and a dollop of plain yogurt or whipped cream, or as an accompaniment to tea or coffee.

1 cup all-purpose flour

1 teaspoon baking powder

1/2 teaspoon salt

1 tablespoon ground cinnamon

1/2 cup (1 stick) unsalted butter, cut into 1/2-inch cubes

1/4 cup sugar

1/2 cup milk

1 egg, lightly beaten

Sugar for sprinkling

Preheat oven to 375°F. Sift the flour, baking powder, salt, and cinnamon into a mixing bowl. Add the butter and mix on medium speed until the butter is cut into small bits and the mixture appears crumbly. With the mixer on low speed, add the sugar and milk and mix until just combined.

Turn the dough out onto a well-floured work surface. Sprinkle some flour over the dough, and use a rolling pin to roll it to 1/2-inch thickness. Cut desired shapes out of the dough, like rounds or squares, and place them 1/2 inch apart on a greased nonstick cookie sheet.

Brush the cookies with beaten egg and sprinkle with sugar. Bake for 16 to 18 minutes, or until they begin to lightly brown around the edges and on top. Remove from oven and allow to cool on the pan or on a wire rack. Store well wrapped or sealed in an airtight container.

Candied Ginger Cookies

*MAKES **25** TO **30** COOKIES*

These unique cookies are simultaneously sweet and spicy, with the refreshing hot bite of ginger. Munch on them in the midafternoon as a vigorous pick-me-up or serve them with Ginger-Vanilla Ice Cream Floats (page 23). They also make tasty accompaniments for iced or hot tea, and many tropical fruit sorbets or ice creams.

1/4 **cup sugar**

1/2 **cup minced gingerroot (about 4 ounces)**

1 **cup (2 sticks) unsalted butter, softened**

3/4 **cup dark brown sugar**

2 **eggs**

2 **cups all-purpose flour**

1 **teaspoon baking powder**

1/2 **teaspoon salt**

1/2 **cup finely ground macadamia nuts or almonds (grind in a food processor)**

Combine the granulated sugar and minced ginger in a sauté pan and place over medium heat. Stir slowly as the sugar melts and the ginger becomes golden and translucent, approximately 6 to 8 minutes. Remove from heat and allow to cool.

In a mixer, cream the butter with the brown sugar. Add the eggs one at a time and mix until well combined. In a separate bowl, sift together the flour, baking powder, and salt and add these dry ingredients to the butter-egg mixture, and mix until combined. Add the nuts and cooled candied ginger and continue mixing until thoroughly combined. Turn the dough out onto a lightly floured work surface and use your hands to roll it into a log shape with a 2 1/2-inch diameter. Wrap it in plastic wrap and refrigerate for at least 1 hour or overnight.

Preheat oven to 375°F. Grease a nonstick cookie sheet. Cut 1/4-inch slices from the chilled log of dough and place them at least 1/2 inch apart on the pan. Bake for 10 to 12 minutes or until lightly browning around the edges. Remove from oven and allow to cool on the pan or on a wire rack. Store well wrapped or sealed in an airtight container.

Gingerbread Cookies

*MAKES **25** TO **30** COOKIES*

Gingerbread has long been a popular European preparation, dating from the 11th century. Each European country has their own favorite variations. This recipe is based on German Pfeffernüsse, a crispy spiced cookie.

1/2 **cup (1 cup) unsalted butter**

1/2 **cup sugar**

1/4 **cup dark brown sugar**

2 **tablespoons honey**

2 **tablespoons molasses**

1/4 **cup milk**

1 1/2 **cups all-purpose flour**

1 **teaspoon baking soda**

2 **teaspoons ground cinnamon**

1/2 **teaspoon ground clove**

2 **teaspoons ground ginger**

In a mixer, cream the butter with the sugar, brown sugar, honey, molasses, and milk. In a separate bowl, sift together the flour, baking soda, and spices. With the mixer on low speed, add the dry ingredients to the butter mixture one cup at a time and mix until well combined. Turn the dough out onto a lightly floured work surface and use your hands to form it into a bricklike shape. Wrap it in plastic wrap and refrigerate for at least 1/2 hour.

Preheat oven to 400°F. Turn the chilled dough out onto a well-floured work surface and sprinkle it with flour. Use a rolling pin to roll it to a thickness of approximately 1/16 inch. Cut desired shapes out of the dough and place them 1 inch apart on a greased nonstick cookie sheet. Bake for 10 to 12 minutes, or until the cookies are well browned. Remove from oven and allow to cool on the pan or on a wire rack. Store well wrapped or sealed in an airtight container.

Had I but a penny in the world, thou shouldst have it for gingerbread.

—WILLIAM SHAKESPEARE

Black Mission Fig–Oatmeal Cookies

MAKES **25** TO **30** COOKIES

This recipe is based on the classic oatmeal raisin cookie, but I've replaced the raisins with delicious rich Black Mission figs. They add a unique, luscious, and decadent quality to these wonderfully moist oatmeal cookies. Just like Grandma made them!

1 cup (2 sticks) unsalted butter, softened

1 1/2 cups dark brown sugar

1 teaspoon salt

2 eggs

2 teaspoons vanilla extract

2 tablespoons milk

2 1/2 cups all-purpose flour

1 1/2 teaspoons baking powder

1 teaspoon baking soda

2 cups rolled oats

1 1/2 cups dried Black Mission figs, roughly chopped

Preheat oven to 350°F. Using a mixer, cream the butter with the brown sugar and salt. In a separate bowl, whisk together the eggs, vanilla, and milk. While mixing on low speed, add the egg mixture to the butter. In a separate bowl, sift together the flour, baking powder, and baking soda. Stir in the rolled oats. With the mixer on low speed, add these dry ingredients to the wet ingredients one cup at a time. Scrape the sides of the bowl with a spatula, and continue mixing until the dough is just combined. Add the chopped figs and mix just enough to evenly distribute them throughout the dough.

Grease a nonstick cookie sheet. Drop the dough on the pan in 2-tablespoon portions at least 2 inches apart. Bake for 15 to 17 minutes, or until the edges of the cookies are lightly browning. Remove from oven and allow to cool on the pan or on a wire rack. Store sealed in an airtight container.

Aniseed Cookies

MAKES **30** TO **35** COOKIES

The mild licorice flavor of aniseed makes a delicious and refreshing cookie. I first tasted aniseed cookies when I bought some in a Middle Eastern specialty store in Chicago. This recipe was inspired by that day of an unexpected cookie discovery! These cookies are crisp and light, excellent accompaniments for ice cream or coffee.

3/4 cup honey

3/4 cup dark brown sugar

1 egg

1/4 cup (1/2 stick) unsalted butter, melted

1 teaspoon baking soda

1 tablespoon ground aniseed

3 cups all-purpose flour

Preheat oven to 375°F. Pour the honey into a saucepan and place over medium heat to warm it just until it loosens in consistency. Pour it into a large bowl and whisk in the brown sugar, egg, and butter. In a separate bowl, sift together the baking soda, aniseed, and flour. Stir the dry mixture into the honey mixture to form a dough.

Turn the dough out onto a well-floured work surface. Cut 1 1/2-inch pieces from the dough and roll them into round balls between the palms of your hands. Place them 2 inches apart on a greased nonstick cookie sheet. Bake for 12 to 14 minutes, or until the cookies are golden brown around the edges. Remove from oven and allow to cool on the pan or on a wire rack. Store well wrapped or sealed in an airtight container.

Giant Fortune Cookies

*MAKES **18** TO **20** COOKIES*

Have fun with fortunes! Use your imagination to create funny or funky personalized fortunes and serve these cookies at your next dinner party—a fantastic source of entertainment and laughs! These thin, crispy spiced cookies are also a delicious treat for ending a meal.

1/2 cup plus 2 tablespoons sugar

1/2 cup plus 2 tablespoons all-purpose flour

1/2 teaspoon ground ginger

1/2 teaspoon ground cinnamon

2 egg whites

1/2 teaspoon vanilla extract

2 tablespoons unsalted butter, melted

18 to 20 fortunes written on 1 1/2 ¥ 1/2-inch strips of paper

Preheat oven to 350°F. Using a mixer equipped with a whisk, whisk together the sugar, flour, ginger, and cinnamon. Add the egg whites and vanilla extract and whisk until smooth. Add the melted butter and mix until thoroughly combined and smooth. Using a metal spatula, spread 1/16-inch-thick circles with 6- to 8-inch diameters on a high-quality nonstick baking sheet.

Bake the circles for 12 to 14 minutes, or until lightly browned. Remove them from the oven and allow to cool for 15 to 20 seconds. Peel a circle from the pan, turn it over, and place a fortune in its center. Fold the bottom edge over the fortune to the top edge and pinch the edges together, creating a half-moon shaped pocket, and then bend the two bottom corners towards each other until they meet. Repeat this process with the remaining circles. If the circles become hardened, you may return them to the oven for 30 to 60 seconds in order to soften them enough to form the cookies. Store in an airtight container.

Caramelized Plantain Curls

*MAKES **20** TO **25** CANDIES*

Here's a delicious and sweet way to prepare green plantains, whose starchy nature makes them resemble potatoes as much as bananas. Drizzle these fried plantains with caramel and dust them with powdered sugar for an unusual and tasty dessert treat! These curls make a wonderful and attractive garnish for ice creams and sorbets.

2 plantains, green and unripe

3 cups vegetable oil for frying

1/2 cup sugar

Powdered sugar for dusting

Peel the plantains and cut in half crosswise. Cut each half lengthwise into 1/16-inch-thick slices. Heat the oil in a large saucepan to 325°F over high heat, then reduce it to low to maintain a hot frying temperature. Fry the plantain slices, 4 or 5 at a time, for 1 1/2 to 2 minutes. Remove them from the oil with a slotted spoon and drain them on paper towels or a flattened paper bag.

Sprinkle the sugar in a sauté pan and place over high heat. Allow the sugar to melt and caramelize, stirring once or twice, until it turns a light amber color. Allow the caramel to cool for 1 minute and then use a spoon to drizzle it evenly over the plantain curls. Sprinkle with powdered sugar. Store in an airtight container.

Honey Almond Tamarind Clusters

*MAKES **20** TO **25** CLUSTERS*

These simple cookie "clusters" are made with tamarind pulp and ground roasted almonds, then lightly tossed in warm honey and rolled in roasted almond slices. The tangy, fruity flavor of tamarind balances out the sweet honey and rich almonds, giving these cookies a real sweet-and-sour character. Tamarind can be purchased fresh in pods or as packaged pulp. If using fresh pods, scrape the pulp from the pods and remove all the seeds.

2 cups sliced almonds

1/4 cup (1/2 stick) unsalted butter

1/2 cup tamarind pulp, seeds removed (2 or 3 pods)

1/2 cup sugar

1 egg

1/2 cup all-purpose flour

1/2 cup honey

Preheat oven to 350°F. Spread the almonds on a dry cookie sheet and roast in the oven for 14 to 16 minutes, or until golden brown. Combine 1 cup of the almonds in a food processor with the butter, tamarind pulp, and sugar and process for 30 seconds. Add the egg and flour and continue processing for 30 seconds, until a thick dough forms.

Prepare a cookie sheet by brushing it lightly with oil or melted butter. Use a tablespoon to drop the dough into small mounds on the pan, at least 1 inch apart from each other. Bake for 16 to 18 minutes or until lightly browned. Remove them from the oven and allow to cool on the pan or on a wire rack.

Warm the honey in a double boiler or bowl over hot water, or by placing the honey still in its container into a pot of hot water. Toss each tamarind cluster in the honey, turning them with a fork to fully coat them, then rolling them in the reserved roasted almonds slices. Store in an airtight container.

Coconut Macaroons

*MAKES **30** TO **35** MACAROONS*

Macaroons are small, round cakes that are crispy on the outside and chewy on the inside, traditionally made with finely ground almonds, sugar, and egg whites. They originated in Italy, and, like the word macaroni, *the name for these popular cakelike cookies is derived from the Italian root* maccherone, *meaning "fine paste." Many French towns are famous for their macaroons, each made in a distinctive style or flavor. Here's a simple recipe for making delicious homemade macaroons with fresh coconut.*

1 coconut

2 egg whites

1 tablespoon sugar

1 cup powdered sugar

Preheat oven to 375°F. Poke a hole in the "eye" of the coconut and drain the water into a bowl, reserving the liquid for another use. Roast the whole coconut in the oven for 20 minutes. Remove the coconut and allow it to cool. Decrease the oven temperature to 350°F. Crack the cooled coconut on a hard surface and pry the flesh from the shell with a large spoon. Use a peeler to make 1/2 cup of coconut shavings from the white flesh.

Whip the egg whites in a mixer at high speed. When they become frothy, sprinkle in the granulated sugar. Continue whipping until stiff peaks form. Sift the powdered sugar into a separate bowl, then stir the grated coconut into it. Fold one-half of the coconut mixture into the whipped whites, then fold in the remaining coconut mixture until just smooth.

Grease a nonstick cookie sheet and dust it liberally with flour, tapping off any excess. Drop the batter by spoonfuls onto the pan, placing them at least 1 inch apart. The macaroons may also be piped onto the pan with a pastry bag equipped with a 1/2-inch plain tip. Bake for 18 to 22 minutes, until golden brown. Remove from the oven and allow to cool on the pan. Store sealed in an airtight container.

Giant Fortune Cookies and Caramelized Plantain Curls

Cinnamon-Raisin Shortbreads

*MAKES **25** TO **30** SHORTBREADS*

Shortbread cookies originated in Scotland, where they were traditionally made with oatmeal and eaten for the Christmas and New Year holidays. For New Year's, shortbread was usually baked in large rounds to symbolize the sun, from which triangular wedges were cut. These delicious, rich shortbreads are flavored with cinnamon—Americans' favorite tropical spice—and raisins, for a delicious cookie to munch in the mornings or any time of day.

3/4 cup (1 1/2 sticks) unsalted butter, softened

1 1/2 cups all-purpose flour

3/4 cup powdered sugar

2 teaspoons ground cinnamon

1/2 teaspoon vanilla extract

1 cup raisins

1 egg white

1/2 cup sugar

Preheat oven to 375°F. In a mixer equipped with a paddle, cream the butter with the flour, powdered sugar, cinnamon, and vanilla. Add the raisins and mix until well distributed throughout the dough.

Turn the dough out onto a lightly floured work surface and cut it in half. Using the palms of your hands, roll the pieces out on the work surface into log shapes with a 1 1/4-inch diameter. Brush the two logs with egg white and roll them in the granulated sugar. Cut the logs crosswise into 1/2-inch-wide slices and place each round slice flat on a greased non-stick cookie sheet. Bake for 16 to 18 minutes or until the shortbreads are just beginning to brown on the edges. Remove from oven and allow to cool. Store in an airtight container.

Pomegranate Shortbreads

*MAKES **30** TO **35** SHORTBREADS*

The crisp, sharp flavors of pomegranate are delicious baked into rich shortbread cookies. The tart seeds of these subtropical fruits provide a perfect balance to these buttery cookies that originated in ancient Scotland.

1 1/4 cups (2 1/2 sticks) unsalted butter, softened

3/4 cup sugar

1/4 teaspoon salt

3 1/4 cups all-purpose flour

1 pomegranate

In a mixer equipped with a paddle, cream the butter, sugar, and salt until lightened in color. Add the flour and mix until it is well worked into the butter mixture.

Slice the pomegranate in half and remove all the juicy red seeds from the white membrane, working over a separate bowl to catch the juice and seeds. Add the pomegranate seeds and juice to the dough and mix gently by hand, folding the dough over itself several times to incorporate and distribute the pomegranate seeds. Turn the dough out onto a lightly floured surface and form it into a brick shape. Wrap it in plastic wrap and refrigerate for 1/2 hour or overnight.

Unwrap the chilled dough and place it on a lightly floured work surface. Cut it into 1/4-inch-thick slices and cut them into desired shapes, such as rectangles or squares. Place them on a cookie sheet that's been lightly brushed with oil or melted butter. Bake for 18 to 20 minutes or until lightly brown around the edges. Remove from oven and allow to cool. Store in an airtight container.

Tempered Bittersweet Chocolate

*FOR DIPPING **35** TO **40** CHOCOLATES*

When chocolate is melted and rehardened, the cocoa butter separates slightly from the cocoa, creating an unappealing dull and dusty surface. Tempering chocolate prevents this, allowing it to cool and harden to a smooth, shiny surface. You will need a batch of tempered chocolate for most of the following chocolate recipes, to be used for dipping the individual chocolates and covering them with an attractive hard shell. When tempering chocolate for the first time, you can use a cooking thermometer to accurately regulate the temperatures.

8 ounces bittersweet chocolate (or semisweet)

Using a sharp chef's knife, roughly cut the chocolate into 1/2-inch pieces and place in a metal bowl or the top part of a double boiler. Place this over a pot of very hot but not boiling water set over low heat. If the water is boiling, or if the chocolate is placed over direct heat, it runs the risk of burning and becoming lumpy. Allow the chocolate to melt, stirring occasionally, and heat the chocolate to a temperature of 125°F, or until it feels very warm to the touch. Remove from the heat and pour half the melted chocolate into a separate bowl and place this in a larger bowl filled with ice water. Return the first bowl of chocolate to the double boiler. Stir the chocolate over ice water until it is cool to the touch (about 82°F) but still of liquid consistency. Stir a small amount of the warm chocolate into the cooled chocolate to slightly increase the temperature until tepid (about 87°F), and return the warm chocolate to the double boiler. The cooled chocolate mixture is now tempered, and ready to use for dipping chocolates. If it cools and thickens while dipping, stir in more warm chocolate to heat it up and loosen its consistency. Unused tempered chocolate may be stored in a covered container and saved for future use.

TEMPERED WHITE CHOCOLATE

Use the same method for tempering white chocolate, except heat it to 118°F instead of 125°F. Lower the temperature to 80°F instead of 82°F, and raise it again to 85°F by adding warm white chocolate.

Peanut Piñon Brittle Florentines

*MAKES **25** TO **30** COOKIES*

Crispy, caramel florentines have always been one of my favorite cookies. They are classically made with almonds, but I think the rich, earthy flavors of peanuts and piñons make a unique and delicious version. Serve these cookies with any flavor ice cream, or with chocolate desserts, like the Bittersweet Chocolate Cake (page 74).

1 cup piñons (pine nuts)

1 cup shelled peanuts

1 cup (2 sticks) unsalted butter

1 3/4 cups sugar

1/2 cup all-purpose flour

1 tablespoon minced orange zest

1 1/4 cups heavy cream

Preheat oven to 350°F. Spread the piñons and peanuts on a dry cookie sheet and roast them in the oven for 12 to 14 minutes, until golden brown. Remove the nuts from the oven and set aside to cool. Leave the oven temperature at 350°F.

Melt the butter in a saucepan over medium heat. Stir in the roasted nuts, sugar, flour, orange zest, and cream. Reduce heat to low and stir continuously for 3 minutes. Remove from heat. Drop the batter in 1-tablespoon mounds at least 3 inches apart on a nonstick cookie sheet. Using the back of a spoon, spread the mounds into 2 1/2-inch-diameter circles. Bake for 16 to 18 minutes, or until golden brown. Remove from the pan while still warm. Store in an airtight container.

Cardamom Chocolates

The contrasting floral and peppery tones of aromatic cardamom are a delicious match for the strong flavor of bittersweet chocolate. These are excellent chocolates to serve with coffee, offering a sweeter interpretation of cardamom-flavored coffee which is popularly served in Arabia.

8 ounces bittersweet chocolate (or semisweet)

3/4 cup heavy cream

1 tablespoon ground cardamom

1 recipe Tempered Bittersweet Chocolate for dipping (page 143, or use semisweet chocolate)

Using a sharp chef's knife, chop the chocolate into small pieces and place it in a large bowl. Combine the cream and cardamom in a saucepan and bring to a boil over medium heat. Watch the boil carefully, making sure the cream doesn't boil up over the edge of the pot. Whisk the hot cream into the bowl of chocolate pieces and stir until all the lumps of chocolate are melted. Brush a 10-inch square pan with oil and line it with plastic wrap. Pour the chocolate cream mixture into the pan and place in the refrigerator to chill and harden.

Cut the chilled chocolate with your chef's knife into desired shapes, such as squares, rectangles, diamonds, or triangles. For smoother edges, warm the knife in hot water between each cut. Place a chocolate on a fork and dip it into the tempered chocolate, scraping excess from the bottom by dragging the fork over the rim of the bowl. Transfer the dipped chocolate to a tray lined with foil or parchment paper, gently sliding it off the fork with a small knife. Repeat the dipping process with each chocolate. Allow them to harden at room temperature. Store in an airtight container in a cool, dry place for up to 3 days, or store them in the refrigerator and allow them to warm to room temperature before serving.

> *What use are cartridges in battle? I always carry chocolates instead.*
>
> —GEORGE BERNARD SHAW

Canela Chocolates

Canela is a type of Mexican cinnamon that is sweeter than other cinnamons, with a softer texture and earthy tones. Cinnamon has long been enjoyed with chocolate in Mexico, dating from Aztec civilization, where it's used to spice liquid chocolate drinks. You can try to locate Mexican dark chocolate for this canela-flavored filling, of which Ibarra is one representative brand.

8 ounces bittersweet chocolate (or semisweet)

3/4 cup heavy cream

1 tablespoon ground canela cinnamon (or ordinary cinnamon)

1 recipe Tempered Bittersweet Chocolate for dipping (page 143, or use semisweet chocolate)

Using a sharp chef's knife, chop the chocolate into small pieces and place it in a large bowl. Combine the cream and canela in a saucepan and bring to a boil over medium heat. Watch the boil carefully, making sure the cream doesn't boil up over the edge of the pot. Whisk the hot cream into the bowl of chocolate pieces and stir until all the lumps of chocolate are melted. Brush a 10-inch square pan with oil and line it with plastic wrap. Pour the chocolate cream mixture into the pan and place in the refrigerator to chill and harden.

Cut the chilled chocolate with a chef's knife into desired shapes, such as squares, rectangles, diamonds, or triangles. For smoother edges, warm the knife in hot water between each cut. Place a chocolate on a fork and dip it into the tempered chocolate, scraping excess from the bottom by dragging the fork over the rim of the bowl. Transfer the dipped chocolate to a tray lined with foil or parchment paper, gently sliding it off the fork with a small knife. Repeat the dipping process with each chocolate. Allow them to harden at room temperature. Store in an airtight container in a cool, dry place for up to 3 days, or store them in the refrigerator and allow them to warm to room temperature before serving.

Banana-Ganache Chocolates

MAKES 25 TO 30 CHOCOLATES

Bananas and chocolate are a spectacular and widely popular flavor combination—remember those beloved banana splits smothered in chocolate sauce? In this recipe, flavor is extracted from the banana peel by simmering it in the cream mixture. The peel is then discarded and fresh pureed bananas are whisked into the mixture along with the chocolate. These delicious treats are sure to be a hit!

8 ounces bittersweet chocolate (or semisweet)

1 banana

1/2 cup heavy cream

1 recipe Tempered Bittersweet Chocolate for dipping (page 143, or use semisweet chocolate)

Using a sharp chef's knife, chop the chocolate into small pieces and place them in a large bowl. Wash and peel the banana and place the peel in a saucepan with the cream. Place over medium-low heat. Puree the banana in a food processor. When the cream comes to a simmer, remove and discard the peel. Whisk the banana puree into the hot cream, increase the heat to medium, and bring the mixture back to a simmer. When it begins to simmer, remove it from the heat and whisk it into the chocolate pieces, stirring until all the chocolate has melted. Brush a 10-inch square pan with oil and line it with plastic wrap. Pour the chocolate cream mixture into the pan and place in the refrigerator to chill and harden.

Cut the chilled chocolate with a chef's knife into desired shapes, such as squares, rectangles, diamonds, or triangles. For smoother edges, warm the knife in hot water between each cut. Place a chocolate on a fork and dip it into the tempered chocolate, scraping excess from the bottom by dragging the fork over the rim of the bowl. Transfer the dipped chocolate to a tray lined with foil or parchment paper, gently sliding it off the fork with a small knife. Repeat the dipping process with each chocolate. Allow them to harden at room temperature. Store in an airtight container in a cool, dry place for up to 3 days, or store them in the refrigerator and allow them to warm to room temperature before serving.

Pecan-Praline Chocolates

MAKES 25 TO 30 CHOCOLATES

Traditionally, praline is a sweet preparation of crushed almonds or hazelnuts coated in caramelized sugar and used as filling in a wide range of pastries, confections, and chocolates. I've used roasted pecans in this recipe, for a unique and rich praline crunch inside each one of these chocolates.

3/4 cup shelled pecans

8 ounces bittersweet chocolate (or semisweet)

1/2 cup sugar

Preheat oven to 350°F. Spread the pecans on a dry cookie sheet and roast them in the oven for 12 to 14 minutes, until golden brown. Remove from the oven and allow to cool.

Using a sharp chef's knife, chop the chocolate into small pieces and place in the top part of a double boiler or a metal bowl over a pot of hot, but not boiling, water. Allow the chocolate to fully melt.

Sprinkle the sugar in a sauté pan and place over high heat. Allow the sugar to melt and caramelize, stirring occasionally with a spoon. When it is amber colored and completely melted, remove it from the heat and stir in the pecans. Pour the mixture onto a lightly oiled cookie sheet and allow it to cool. When cooled, place the pecan caramel into a food processor and pulverize it until finely ground. Whisk this into the melted chocolate until well combined. Line a 10-inch square pan with plastic wrap and pour the chocolate mixture into it. Place in the refrigerator for at least 30 minutes, or until well set. Cut the chilled chocolate with a sharp chef's knife into desired shapes, such as squares, rectangles, or diamonds. Store in an airtight container.

Kumquat Chocolates

*MAKES **35** TO **40** CHOCOLATES*

The bitter orange nature of kumquats is an excellent match for smooth, bittersweet chocolate.

35 to 40 kumquats

7 cups water

2 cups sugar

8 ounces bittersweet chocolate (or semisweet)

1/2 cup heavy cream

1/4 cup orange liqueur, such as Grand Marnier or Cointreau

1 recipe Tempered Bittersweet Chocolate for dipping (page 143) (optional)

Trim about 1/8 inch off the stem ends of the kumquats. Place the kumquats and 4 cups of water in a saucepan over medium heat. Simmer for 20 to 25 minutes. Drain this water off, retaining the fruit in the pot, and add the remaining 3 cups of water to the pot along with 2 cups of the sugar. Return to medium heat and simmer for 35 to 40 minutes. Drain off the syrup and allow the kumquats to cool. Squeeze out and discard the inner pulp and seeds from the insides of the kumquats. Set the candied, hollowed out kumquats aside.

Chop the chocolate into small pieces and place in a large bowl. Combine the cream and orange liqueur in a saucepan and bring to a boil over medium heat. Make sure the cream doesn't boil up over the edge of the pan. Whisk the hot cream into the bowl of chocolate pieces and stir until the chocolate is melted. Place the bowl in the refrigerator and allow to cool, stirring periodically, until the chocolate thickens to the point where soft peaks remain standing if you lift the spoon out of the bowl.

Transfer the cooled chocolate to a pastry bag equipped with a 1/4- or 3/8-inch plain tip, and fill the candied kumquats. Allow them to cool and fully set for about 15 minutes. If desired, you may then dip the kumquats and cover them halfway with a shiny coating of bittersweet tempered chocolate. Hold the bottom half of the kumquat with your fingers and dip the cut, filled ends into the tempered chocolate. Place them on a cookie sheet lined with aluminum foil and allow to harden.

Espresso-Bean Chocolates

*MAKES **25** TO **30** CHOCOLATES*

Everyone loves the combined flavors of coffee and chocolate, and these rich chocolates give you a burst of each in every bite! Finely ground espresso beans are simmered in the cream to give these delicacies a lingering, complex, but perfectly integrated coffee-chocolate flavor.

8 ounces bittersweet chocolate (or semisweet)

3/4 cup heavy cream

1/4 cup finely ground espresso or coffee beans

Cocoa powder for dusting

Using a sharp chef's knife, chop the chocolate into small pieces and place in a large bowl. Combine the cream and finely ground espresso beans in a saucepan and bring to a boil over medium heat. Watch carefully, making sure the cream doesn't boil up over the edge of the pan. Whisk the hot cream into the bowl of chocolate pieces and stir until all the lumps of chocolate are melted. Place the bowl in the refrigerator or over an ice bath and allow to cool, stirring periodically, until the chocolate thickens to the point where soft peaks remain standing if you lift the spoon out of the bowl.

Transfer the cooled chocolate to a pastry bag equipped with a 1/2-inch plain tip. Pipe 1/2-inch mounds onto a cookie sheet lined with aluminum foil or parchment paper. Chill the mounds in the refrigerator for 15 minutes. Roll the mounds between the palms of your hands to create oval shapes. Using the back of a paring knife, make indentations lengthwise on the ovals by pressing one-quarter of the way into the chocolates, so that they resemble whole coffee beans. Return them to the refrigerator and chill again for a few minutes. Toss the chocolates in a small bowl of cocoa powder, tapping off any excess. Store in an airtight container.

Chocolates (clockwise from top right): Kumquat, Candied Grapefruit, Espresso-Bean, Banana-Ganache, and Starfruit

Candied Grapefruit Chocolates

*MAKES **25** TO **30** CHOCOLATES*

For these chocolates, strips of grapefruit rind are candied in a simple syrup, dipped in tempered bittersweet chocolate, and then rolled in an allspice–powdered sugar mixture. The intense, complementary flavors of grapefruit and allspice make these chocolates stand out from the crowd!

Rind from 1/2 grapefruit

6 cups water

2 1/2 cups sugar

1 tablespoon powdered sugar

1 tablespoon ground allspice

1 recipe Tempered Bittersweet Chocolate for dipping (page 143, or use semisweet chocolate)

Cut the grapefruit rind into strips 1/4 inch wide and 2 inches long. Place them in a saucepan with 3 cups water and bring to a boil over medium heat. Reduce the heat slightly and maintain a low boil for 25 minutes. Drain the water from the grapefruit and return the fruit to the pot with the remaining 4 cups water and the sugar and place over medium heat. Bring to a boil, reduce heat to low, and simmer until the grapefruit strips are candied and translucent, about 40 to 45 minutes. Pass through a fine strainer to drain the sugar syrup from the candied grapefruit, and spread the strips on a cookie sheet to cool. When thoroughly cooled, pat them with a paper towel to remove any excess syrup.

In a small bowl, stir together the powdered sugar and allspice. Place a candied grapefruit rind on a fork and dip it into tempered chocolate, dragging the fork over the rim of the bowl to remove excess chocolate. Drop the chocolate-covered rind into the sugar-allspice mixture and roll to coat it well. Place it on a cookie sheet lined with aluminum foil or parchment paper and allow to harden. Repeat dipping and rolling process for each candied grapefruit rind. Store in an airtight container.

Starfruit Chocolates

*MAKES **30** TO **35** CHOCOLATES*

Fruit dipped in chocolate is one of the most simple and satisfying chocolate pleasures! Although strawberries are usually favored for dipping in chocolate, I think starfruits are a delicious tropical alternative. Their luscious, tart flavor provides a pleasing and refreshing counterpoint to the sweet chocolate coating.

3 carambola (starfruits)

1 recipe Tempered Bittersweet Chocolate or Tempered White Chocolate for dipping (page 143, or use semisweet chocolate)

Cut the starfruits in half lengthwise and use the point of a sharp paring knife to remove any visible seeds along the center core. Cut the halves crosswise into 1/4-inch-thick slices. Pat the slices dry with a paper towel. Holding the slices with your fingers, dip them halfway into the tempered chocolate and place on a cookie sheet lined with aluminum foil or parchment paper. Allow to harden. Store covered in the refrigerator.

Sour Kiwi White Chocolates

*MAKES **30** CHOCOLATES*

This recipe is made especially for white chocolate lovers—the acidic nature of slightly underripe kiwis can really stand up to the sweetness of white chocolate, giving these simple treats a well-balanced combination of flavors.

5 kiwis, slightly underripe

1 recipe Tempered White Chocolate for dipping (page 143)

Using a sharp paring knife, peel the kiwis and remove the hard stem from the end. Cut them in half lengthwise and then cut each half lengthwise into 3 equally sized wedges. Pat the wedges with a paper towel to remove excess moisture from the freshly cut fruit. Holding the wedges with your fingers, dip them halfway into the tempered chocolate and place on a cookie sheet lined with aluminum foil or parchment paper. Allow to harden. Store covered in the refrigerator.

Macadamia-Nougat Caramels

MAKES **20** *TO* **25** *CANDIES*

Sweet nougat dates from ancient Roman times, when it was called nucatum and made with honey, eggs, and walnuts. Around 1650, France became the largest manufacturing center of nougat, using almonds instead of walnuts. Here's my own tropical version of nougat, with a rich caramelized nougat rolled while still warm in delicately flavored roasted macadamia nuts.

1 cup macadamia nuts

1/2 cup hot water

2 tablespoons butter, melted

1/2 cup heavy cream

1 1/2 cups sugar

Preheat oven to 350°F. Spread the macadamia nuts on a cookie sheet and roast in the oven for 14 to 16 minutes, until golden brown. Remove from the oven and allow to cool. Line an 8×8×4-inch loaf pan with aluminum foil and lightly brush it with oil.

Combine the water, butter, and cream in a bowl and stir together. Set aside. Sprinkle the sugar in a large sauté pan and place over medium heat. Allow the sugar to melt and caramelize until amber colored, then remove it from the heat. Stir the water-cream mixture into the amber-colored caramel, taking special care as it may initially splatter and pop, until the caramel has completely dissolved. Return the mixture to the heat and bring to a boil. Allow to simmer for approximately 6 minutes. Pour the mixture into the foil-lined pan and allow to cool.

When the caramel begins to harden, remove it from the pan and peel off the foil. Cut it into 3/4-inch squares. Crush the roasted macadamia nuts lightly with the side of a chef's knife. Roll the caramel squares between your palms to form round balls, then roll them in the crushed roasted nuts. Store in an airtight container.

Brazil Nut–Marzipan Chocolates

MAKES **20** *TO* **25** *CHOCOLATES*

Marzipan is traditionally a thick paste made with ground almonds, egg whites, and sugar or sugar syrup. Here I replace the almonds with roasted Brazil nuts and dip the candies into tempered bittersweet chocolate. The earthy tones of roasted Brazil nuts are an excellent match for chocolate, making these tempting treats irresistible.

2 cups shelled Brazil nuts

1/2 cup light corn syrup

1/4 cup powdered sugar

1 recipe Tempered Bittersweet Chocolate (page 143, or use semisweet chocolate)

Preheat oven to 350°F. Spread the Brazil nuts on a dry cookie sheet and roast in the oven for 14 to 16 minutes, until golden brown. Remove from the oven and allow to cool briefly. Place the roasted nuts in a food processor and pulverize for 30 seconds. Add the corn syrup and powdered sugar, and continue pulverizing until a stiff mass forms. For this recipe, this mixture is called marzipan.

Turn the marzipan out onto a work surface that's lightly dusted with powdered sugar, and cut it into 1-inch pieces. Roll the pieces between the palms of your hands first into rounds and then into oval shapes with slightly pointed ends bent inwards, trying to emulate the natural shape of the Brazil nuts. Holding the marzipan "nuts" with your fingers, dip them halfway into the tempered chocolate and place them on a cookie sheet lined with aluminum foil or parchment paper. Allow to harden. Store in an airtight container.

Orange-Allspice Jellies

*MAKES **30** TO **35** CANDIES*

Dessert jellies are traditionally made from fruit juice, wine, or liqueurs that are sweetened and then gelatinized. These jellies are made with oranges and allspice, always an excellent flavor complement to citrus fruits, and then lightly coated with granulated sugar. Jellies are quick and simple candies to make, but you must be sure to allow sufficient refrigeration time before serving so they can fully gel.

6 oranges

2 teaspoons ground allspice

4 teaspoons powdered unflavored gelatin (2 packets)

2 tablespoons cold water

Granulated sugar for coating

Using a sharp chef's knife, trim the tops and bottoms off the oranges, then cut all the peel and pith from the inner flesh, working your way around the fruit. Section the oranges by cutting between each membrane and removing each tender wedge of fruit, working over a bowl to catch any dripping juices. When all the sections are removed, squeeze as much juice as possible from the membrane.

Add the allspice to the orange segments and juice, and pour the mixture into a food processor. Pulse several times to break up the orange flesh. Transfer the mixture to a saucepan and bring to a boil over medium heat. Lower the heat slightly to maintain a low boil for 15 minutes, until the juice has reduced a little bit and intensified its flavor. While the juice is boiling, sprinkle the gelatin into the cold water in a small bowl and allow to sit for 5 minutes to "bloom." When the juice is slightly reduced, remove it from the heat and whisk in the gelatin water for 3 to 4 minutes until completely dissolved. Pour this mixture into a 10-inch square pan that's been lightly brushed with oil and lined with plastic wrap. Refrigerate for at least 2 hours. Remove from the pan and cut into squares, triangles, or other desired shapes. Toss the candies in granulated sugar. Store in an airtight container, refrigerated.

Persimmon-Canela Jellies

*MAKES **30** TO **35** CANDIES*

These candies make delicious use of persimmons, which are a very seasonal spring fruit. Their delicate flavor resembles a combination of plums, pumpkins, and honey. Be sure to only use persimmons that are very ripe and jelly-soft to the touch.

6 persimmons

1/2 cup sugar

2 teaspoons ground canela cinnamon (or regular cinnamon)

4 teaspoons powdered unflavored gelatin (2 packets)

2 tablespoons cold water

Granulated sugar for coating

Cut the top stems from the persimmons and slice them in half. Remove the pits and place in a food processor with the sugar and canela. Puree until smooth, approximately 30 seconds.

In a small bowl, sprinkle the gelatin into the cold water and allow to sit for 5 minutes. Pour the persimmon puree into a saucepan and simmer over medium heat. Remove from the heat and whisk in the "bloomed" gelatin for 3 to 4 minutes until it's completely dissolved. Pour mixture into a 10-inch square pan that's been lightly brushed with oil and lined with plastic wrap. Refrigerate for at least 2 hours. Remove from the pan, cut into desired shapes, and toss in granulated sugar. Refrigerate in an airtight container.

> *Deep within Saga valley*
> *facing the mountain*
> *companion to birds and fish*
> *this sweet wilderness could be*
> *some old hermit's dwelling.*
> *No "red dragon's eyes"*
> *on the tips of the persimmon,*
> *but the leaves provide poetic themes*
> *and are conducive to learning.*
> —MATSUO BASHO, FROM *THE SAGA DIARY* (1691)

Date-Pistachio Cookies

*MAKES **25** TO **30** COOKIES*

The palm trees on which dates grow were a source of natural wealth in ancient Persia, Arabia, Mesopotamia, and North Africa because every part of the wood, leaves, sap, and fruit was used by humans. These cookies celebrate an ancient flavor combination from these regions, where dates and pistachios have been paired together in both sweet and savory foods for hundreds of years.

12 to 14 dates, pitted and roughly chopped

1/2 cup (1 stick) unsalted butter

1/4 cup dark brown sugar

2 teaspoons vanilla extract

2 cups shelled pistachios

2 cups all-purpose flour

Preheat oven to 375°F. In a mixer equipped with a paddle, cream together the dates, butter, brown sugar, and vanilla for 2 minutes. Pulverize the pistachios with the flour in a food processor until the nuts are finely ground. With the mixer on low speed, add the nut-flour mixture one cup at a time to the date mixture and mix until smooth.

Turn the dough out onto a floured work surface, sprinkle it with flour, and use a rolling pin to roll it to a thickness of 1/4 inch. Cut out desired shapes and place them 1 inch apart on a cookie sheet or cookie pan that has been brushed lightly with oil or melted butter. Bake for 16 to 18 minutes. Remove from oven allow to cool on the pan or on a wire rack. Store in an airtight container.

Tamarillo Jellies

*MAKES **30** TO **35** CANDIES*

The red to apricot-colored flesh of tamarillos gives these candies an attractive and enticing hue. Their tart and acidic nature also lends itself to jellies, providing a burst of flavor that is nicely balanced by this sweet preparation.

8 tamarillos

1 1/2 cups sugar

4 teaspoons powdered unflavored gelatin (2 packets)

2 tablespoons cold water

Granulated sugar for coating

Cut the tamarillos in half lengthwise and use a spoon to scoop all the flesh from the thick skins into a food processor. Add the sugar and puree for 30 seconds, or until smooth. Pass the mixture through a fine strainer to remove the seeds.

In a separate small bowl, sprinkle the gelatin into the cold water and allow to sit for 5 minutes to "bloom." Pour the tamarillo puree into a saucepan and bring to a simmer over medium heat. Remove from the heat and whisk in the bloomed gelatin for 3 to 4 minutes until it's completely dissolved. Pour this mixture into a 10-inch square pan that's been lightly brushed with oil and lined with plastic wrap. Refrigerate for at least 2 hours. Remove from the pan and cut into desired shapes. Toss the candies in granulated sugar. Store in an airtight container.

Resources

If you have trouble finding some of the tropical and subtropical ingredients called for in these recipes in your local super-markets, natural food stores, and specialty stores, they can be ordered through the mail. Use this source guide to help you find the right company for the products you want.

TROPICAL AND SUBTROPICAL FRUITS

Florida Sunshine Groves
5637 Gall Boulevard
Zephyrhills, FL 34248
800/527-9917
813/782-4816
Assorted citrus fruits

Valley Cove Ranch
P.O. Box 603
Springville, CA 93265
209/539-2710
Organically grown citrus fruits

Pittman and Davis
P.O. Box 2227
Harlingen, TX 78551
512/423-2154
Assorted citrus fruits, pineapples, mangoes, and kiwi

Frieda's Finest
P.O. Box 58488
Los Angeles, CA 90058
800/421-9477
213/627-2981
Assorted tropical fruits

Brooks Tropicals
P.O. Box 900160
Homestead, FL 33090
800/327-4833
Assorted tropical fruits

Seaside Banana Garden
6823 Santa Barbara Avenue
La Conchita, CA 93001
805/643-4061
Assorted banana varieties, including Ladyfinger baby bananas and red bananas

Green Hills Farms
P.O. Box 663
Temecula, CA 92390
No phone orders ($13 for 6 to 7 pounds)
Assorted persimmon varieties

Oasis Date Gardens
P.O. Box 757
59-111 Highway 111
Thermal, CA 92274
619/399-5665
Assorted date varieties

TROPICAL AND SUBTROPICAL NUTS

Fiesta Nuts
P.O. Box 366
75 Harbor Road
Port Washington, NY 11050
800/645-3296
516/883-1403
Cashews, almonds, pistachios, and macadamias; also figs

Almond Plaza
P.O. Box 500
Sacramento, CA 95803-0500
800/225-NUTS
Almonds

Hawaiian Plantations
802 Lehua Avenue
Pearl City, HI 96782
808/456-7078
Macadamias

Green Valley Country Estate Pecans
1625 E. Helmet Peak
Sahuarita, AZ 85629
800/327-3226
602/791-2062
Pecans

Señor Murphy
P.O. Box 2505
Santa Fe, NM 87504-2505
505/988-4311
New Mexican piñons (pine nuts)

TROPICAL SPICES

San Francisco Herb Company
250 14th Street
San Francisco, CA 94103
800/227-4530
800/622-0768 within CA
415/861-7174
Assorted exotic spices

Rafal Spice Company
2521 Russell Street
Detroit, MI 48207
313/259-6373
Assorted exotic spices

Meadowbrook Herb Garden
R.R. Box 138
Wyoming, RI 02898
401/539-7603
Unradiated, unfumigated imported spices and organically grown herbs

Vanilla Saffron Imports
70 Manchester Street
San Francisco, CA 94110
415/648-8990
High-quality vanilla beans

Bibliography

Bilheux, Roland, and Alain Escoffier. *Petits Fours, Chocolate, Frozen Desserts, and Sugar Work.* New York: Van Nostrand Reinhold, 1985.

Blue Goose Growers. *The Buying Guide: For Fresh Fruits, Vegetables, Herbs and Nuts.* 1986.

Brillat-Savarin, Jean Anthelme. *The Physiology of Taste.* Translated by M. F. K. Fisher. New York: The Heritage Press, 1949.

Burnett, Paula, ed. *The Penguin Book of Caribbean Verse in English.* Middlesex, England: Penguin Books, 1986.

Cruz, V. H., L. V. Quintana, and V. Suarez, eds. *Paper Dance: 55 Latino Poets.* New York: Persea Books, 1995.

de Baralt, Blanche Z. *Cuban Cookery: Gastronomic Secrets of the Tropics.* Havana, Cuba: Molina and Cia, 1945(?).

Forsyth, Adrian. *How Monkeys Make Chocolate: Foods and Medicines from the Rainforests.* Toronto: Owl Books, 1995.

Friberg, Bo. *The Professional Pastry Chef.* 3d ed. New York: Van Nostrand Reinhold, 1996.

Hass, Robert, ed. *The Essential Haiku.* Hopewell, N.J.: Ecco Press, 1994.

Holmes, Christine. *Captain Cook's Final Voyage: The Journal of Midshipman George Gilbert.* Honolulu: University Press of Hawaii, 1982.

Lang, Jennifer Harvey, ed. *Larousse Gastronomique.* New York: Crown Publishers, 1988.

MacLauchlan, Andrew. *New Classic Desserts.* New York: Van Nostrand Reinhold, 1995.

Masefield, John, ed. *The Travels of Marco Polo.* London: J. M. Dent and Sons, 1958.

Melville, Herman. *Typee: A Peep at Polynesian Life.* Evanston, Ill.: Northwestern University Press, 1968.

Miller, Mark. *Coyote Cafe.* Berkeley: Ten Speed Press, 1989.

Mortensen, Ernest, and Ervin T. Bullard. *Handbook of Tropical and Subtropical Horticulture.* Washington, D.C.: Agency for International Development, 1970.

Parry, John W. *Spices.* New York: Chemical Publishing Company, 1971.

Pigafetta, Antonio. *Magellan's Voyage: A Narrative Account of the First Circumnavigation.* New Haven: Yale University Press, 1969.

Ritchie, Carson I. A. *Food in Civilisation: How History has been Affected by Human Tastes.* New York: Beaufort Books, 1981.

Rodriguez, Douglas. *Nuevo Latino.* Berkeley: Ten Speed Press, 1995.

Schneider, Elizabeth. *Uncommon Fruits and Vegetables: A Commonsense Guide.* New York: Harper & Row, 1986.

Trager, James. *The Food Chronology: A Food Lover's Compendium of Events and Anecdotes, from Prehistory to the Present.* New York: Henry Holt and Company, 1995.

Van Aken, Norman. *The Great Exotic Fruit Book.* Berkeley: Ten Speed Press, 1995.

Ward, Artemis. *The Encyclopedia of Food.* New York: Artemis Ward, 1923.

Wiegand, Lee. *Food Catalog: The Ultimate Guide to Buying Food by Mail.* New York: Clarkson Potter, 1990.

Index